D1573260

THE STOCK MARKET
CRASH OF 1929
THE END OF PROSPERITY

MILESTONES
IN
AMERICAN HISTORY
★★★★★★★★★★★★★★★

THE STOCK MARKET CRASH OF 1929

THE END OF PROSPERITY

BRENDA LANGE

CHELSEA HOUSE
PUBLISHERS
An imprint of Infobase Publishing

The Stock Market Crash of 1929: The End of Prosperity

Copyright © 2007 by Infobase Publishing

Chelsea House
An imprint of Infobase Publishing
132 West 31st Street
New York, NY 10001

ISBN 10: 0-7910-9354-9
ISBN 13: 978-0-7910-9354-2

Library of Congress Cataloging-in-Publication Data
Lange, Brenda.
  The Stock Market Crash of 1929 : the end of prosperity / Brenda Lange.
    p. cm. — (Milestones in American history)
  Includes bibliographical references and index.
  ISBN 0-7910-9354-9 (hardcover)
  1. Stock Market Crash, 1929—Juvenile literature. 2. Depressions—1929—United States—Juvenile literature. 3. United States—Economic conditions—1918-1945—Juvenile literature. I. Title. II. Series.

  HB37171929 L23 2007
  332.64'27309042—dc22   2006038868

Series design by Erik Lindstrom
Cover design by Ben Peterson

Printed in the United States of America

Bang NMSG 10 9 8 7 6 5 4 3 2 1

CONTENTS

The End of
an Era

Thousands packed the streets of New York City's financial district. Anxious investors had heard rumblings throughout the day about mass panic on Wall Street, with rampant selling of stocks causing values to plummet. Rumors swirled around the crowd like snowflakes in a blizzard. The date was Tuesday, October 29, 1929—what would forever be known as "Black Tuesday."

During the 1920s, people were content and the future seemed promising. The horrors of World War I were in the past and happy days were here again. As sons came marching home from the war, the production of luxury items increased. Refrigerators, radios, cars—all items the average consumer wanted and "had to have"—were often bought using borrowed money. Buying on credit was a fairly new concept, because most Americans had always preferred to pay cash for purchases. Banks were eager to lend money for these goods and became just as willing to extend credit for the purchase of stocks.

Companies can be owned privately or publicly. If a company is owned privately, it does not sell stock to the public; if it is owned publicly, it does. A stock, also called a share, is a piece of the ownership of a company. Anyone can buy a share of a company. Businesses and corporations sell shares of ownership because it is an easy way for them to make money. When you buy a share in a company, you become a part owner, proportionate to the amount of stock you own. The more stock you hold in a company, the more invested you are in its success. If a person buys a share at a low price, and the price of the stock goes up, that person has made money. The key to making money on the stock market is to buy stocks when the prices are low and sell those stocks to others when the prices have climbed. Investing in stocks seemed like a good way to make money. Many people were so convinced that they could get rich by investing in the stock market, they often borrowed heavily to buy more stock, and from 1920 to 1929 stocks more than quadrupled in value.

As stock prices continued to climb throughout the 1920s, many investors came to believe that stocks were a sure way to ensure a secure future for their families. It is estimated that of the $50 billion in new shares offered during the 1920s, half became worthless by 1930. Banks were among the biggest players, and when the market crashed, people were afraid the banks would not have any cash for them if they wanted to withdraw their money. This fear led many to empty their accounts. This mass withdrawal was called a "run" on the banks and caused many of them to go out of business.

Borrowing money to buy stock—known as buying on margin—became commonplace. And it wasn't only the rich executive who bought stock. The average blue-collar worker was able to borrow money to buy stock against the future value of that stock. This widespread practice of buying on margin is considered to be one of the primary causes of the market's

BLACK TUESDAY

The following excerpt is from an October 30, 1929, *New York Times* article that illustrates the hopeless feeling experienced by stock traders during Black Tuesday. Although investors began trading large quantities of stock on Thursday, October 24, which is often dubbed "Black Thursday," the real panic did not begin until Monday, October 28, when the market dropped 12.8 percent from the previous Friday. The next day, October 29, the market fell another 12 percent, as more than 16 million shares were traded in the most cataclysmic day in the history of the stock market. At the time, the *New York Times* estimated that between $8 and $9 million was lost on Black Tuesday.

Groups of men, with here and there a woman, stood about inverted glass bowls all over the city yesterday watching spools of ticker tape unwind and as the tenuous paper with its cryptic numerals grew longer at their feet their fortunes shrunk. Others sat stolidly on tilted chairs in the customers' rooms of brokerage houses and watched a motion picture of waning wealth as the day's quotations moved silently across a screen.

It was among such groups as these, feeling the pulse of a feverish financial world whose heart is the Stock Exchange, that drama and perhaps tragedy were to be found . . . the crowds about the ticker tape, like friends around the bedside of a stricken friend, reflected in their faces the story the tape was telling. There were no smiles. There were no tears either. Just the camaraderie of fellow-sufferers. Everybody wanted to tell his neighbor how much he had lost. Nobody wanted to listen. It was too repetitious a tale.*

---

* "Stocks Collapse in 16,410,030-Share Day, but Rally at Close Cheers Brokers; Bankers Optimistic, to Continue Aid," *New York Times,* October 30, 1929.

eventual crash. There was, however, an underlying weakness in the economy, and so the crash is seen as the beginning of the Great Depression era, not its cause. A record 16.4 million shares were traded on Black Tuesday, and the market lost about 12 percent. Events in the months leading up to that Tuesday—including buying on margin and other practices—had given some people reason to believe the market's upward spiral was about to reverse itself. But even highly respected economists, businessmen, and bankers were caught up in a frenzy of speculating in stocks, and ignored some subtle clues. Even the most educated investors lost fortunes. It is generally accepted that October 29, 1929, was the last day of the carefree Roaring Twenties and the beginning of the Great Depression.

While the crash affected rich and poor investors alike, most of the people who lost money were urban dwellers. There were, however, ripple effects of this sharp economic downturn, which quickly extended into rural areas and worsened an already dangerous situation there. There had been an ongoing agricultural depression during the 1920s, which intensified as farm prices dropped due to overemployment within the industry. After the Great Depression began, the shortage of work and cash spread from the farmlands to the cities and back again in the aftermath of the crash. By 1933, the year Franklin D. Roosevelt was sworn in as president, the average American's salary had fallen about 40 percent, to about $1,500 a year, and the unemployment rate stood at 25 percent, or about 13 million people. Those who lost their jobs were often those who could least afford to—those already at the bottom of the economic ladder.

A laborer in New York City, for example, with a wife and several children at home to support, would have had little or no savings. When production slowed and he lost his job, there was nothing to fall back on. And if he had borrowed money to invest in the stock market, hoping to strike it rich, he would have to sell any personal items he could to pay back those

Many American people blamed President Herbert Hoover for the dire economic conditions experienced during the Great Depression. As a result, the homeless and jobless named the shantytowns they were forced to build "Hoovervilles," because they believed the president did little to help bring the country out of its disastrous economic situation. Here, two Hooverville children are pictured next to signs that further mock the president.

loans. Thousands of families found themselves in this situation and were evicted from their homes and forced to rely on the kindnesses of relatives, or set up housekeeping on the streets. Hundreds of shantytowns sprang up throughout the country, populated by the newly homeless. Mockingly named "Hoovervilles" after President Herbert Hoover, who was thought to be indifferent to the suffering and unwilling (or unable) to help alleviate it, these temporary housing developments were breeding grounds for despair.

The social changes experienced during the Great Depression were far reaching and long lasting. One of the enormous impacts was on family structure and roles. The traditional view, that the man was the income provider, often changed because he could not always find work. But his wife and children might find small jobs to bring home enough money for the family to scrape by. This role reversal put a strain on families, leaving them confused and frustrated. Families were often split—children were often sent to live with relatives, while their parents survived the best they could. Sometimes men simply could not handle the hurt and anxiety, and left altogether to join other men riding the country's railway system in search of a better life.

And men were not the only ones who took to the road. Boys, and sometimes girls, joined them out of necessity. Sometimes a family simply could not feed all of its children and sent the oldest one out to fend for himself. Life on the road was tough, but these "hobos" survived by living together, forming what passed as families for them during their time away from home.

During the early 1930s, a severe drought affected the Plains states, which forced many farmers and their families to migrate en masse toward the cities. Areas of Oklahoma, Colorado, Kansas, and Texas experienced such prolonged drought that the area became known as the "Dust Bowl" and its inhabitants headed westward in droves. Chronicled in John Steinbeck's classic novel *The Grapes of Wrath*, these families often ended up as migrant workers in California's fruit orchards and vegetable fields. The "Okies" were not the only ones to migrate. Thousands of blacks moved from the South to northern cities, and millions of Mexican and Filipino immigrants returned to their homelands.

Traditional American optimism could only carry the country so far. As the Great Depression dragged on, despair grew deeper. Perhaps no event in the country's history had such an encompassing effect on mass feelings and thoughts—the ways Americans thought of themselves—since the Civil War.

THE U.S. GOVERNMENT'S REACTION

Prior to October 1929, the average American had very little to do with the federal government, nor the government with him or her. President Calvin Coolidge (who served from 1923–1929) once said that the average American would not notice if the government disappeared for six months. That was an exaggeration, of course, but before the stock market crashed, the government's primary involvement in people's lives was through the post office and services for war veterans.

But by the end of the Great Depression, generally considered to be around 1941, when America entered World War II, there were dozens of federally mandated programs in place to provide work, to help ease Americans' suffering, to regulate the activities of the banking industry and stock exchanges, and to regulate business practices. One of the most important social programs was created by the Social Security Administration in 1935. Social Security was originally established not only as a financial safety net for old age but also as an unemployment insurance benefit that was overseen by the federal and state governments jointly. Before its institution, states and private agencies had provided some relief to orphans, widows, and the homeless, but there was no national system in place. These smaller agencies could not handle the sheer volume of the destitute arriving daily at their doors. The Social Security Act provided an additional level of security and stability that had not been experienced before.

THE NEW DEAL

The package of programs and laws instituted by President Roosevelt's administration is known as the "New Deal." This phrase encompasses a wide range of initiatives, some of which were

In 1932, Franklin Roosevelt was overwhelmingly elected the thirty-second president of the United States, winning by a margin of more than 7 million votes and carrying all but six states. Roosevelt endeared himself to U.S. citizens by engaging in "fireside chats," which were regular national radio broadcasts that brought Roosevelt's voice straight into people's living rooms.

successful, and others that did not fare as well. Roosevelt used the power of his charismatic personality to sell the American public on these new programs, getting them to join him in his "great experiment." He did that in person and through weekly radio addresses that were known as "fireside chats." Millions sat raptly in front of their radios each week listening to his strong voice encourage, inform, and reassure.

The American people had supported Roosevelt in 1932 in droves, helping him gain an overwhelming victory in the presidential election over his opponent, Herbert Hoover. Roosevelt won 42 out of 48 states. He brought a measure of hope back to the country in his inaugural address when he promised to put people back to work and uttered that now famous phrase, "We have nothing to fear but fear itself."

Two well-known programs Roosevelt established were the Works Progress Administration (WPA), which put thousands to work (mostly widows or women whose husbands were disabled), and the Civilian Conservation Corps (CCC), which put thousands of young men to work on projects such as building roads and dams and planting trees. The Tennessee Valley Authority (TVA) also put thousands to work building dams and bringing electricity to that region. Together these work programs employed millions during the Great Depression and in the process were responsible for the creation of much-needed infrastructures (roads, dams, bridges) and public buildings (schools and libraries).

Of course, not everyone agreed with Roosevelt's New Deal policies. They felt that some of his programs would lead to a welfare state in which people would grow lazy and sit around collecting government "paychecks." Although Hoover was an exception, most conservative Republicans believed that the government should retain its former "laissez-faire" or "leave-alone" policies and let the people fend for themselves. They felt that reliance on government help would weaken the people's character and ultimately the fabric of the entire country. In fact, Hoover had made a speech earlier in 1929, in which he uttered the words that have become associated with the Republican belief system. He said that Americans had always been known for their "rugged individualism" and it was that independent confidence and can-do attitude that would pull the country through any storm—not direct government intervention.

Whether one supported or opposed Roosevelt's New Deal policies, his programs employed millions in a time of need, put money back in their pockets, and food back on the table. These programs also worked in an intangible way to restore a sense of confidence and faith in the future. Most of these policies remained in place throughout each of Roosevelt's administrations (he was reelected in 1936, 1940, and 1944). But it took an event out of Roosevelt's control to truly turn the nation's economy around. When the United States entered World War II, factory and farm production increased in order to

HERBERT CLARK HOOVER
(1874–1964)

The Scapegoat for the Great Depression

Herbert Hoover was the thirty-first president of the United States, entering office months before the stock market crash of October 29, 1929, and leaving at the height of the Great Depression in 1933.

He was born to Quaker parents in a village in Iowa, where his father was a blacksmith. Orphaned at the age of nine, he grew up with relatives in Oregon and attended Stanford University in California, where he studied engineering. It was there he met his wife, Lou Henry. Later on, the two traveled to China, where a private mining company hired Hoover as head engineer.

From there, the couple traveled to London, where they were living when Germany declared war on France in 1914. Hoover subsequently helped ease suffering abroad as the head of the Commission for the Relief of Belgium during the war. His organization and leadership earned him the reputation of being a great humanitarian. He served during the 1920s as U.S. secretary of commerce, and when accepting the Republican presidential nomination in 1928, said, "We in America today are nearer to the final triumph over poverty provide supplies for troops overseas. This created millions of additional jobs, energized the U.S. economy, and effectively ended the Great Depression.

The pendulum swung in a wide arc from the optimistic Roaring Twenties to the tragedy of Black Tuesday and on through the struggle of the Great Depression. What was the country like before, during, and after? What did it take to rebuild fortunes and recreate what had been lost? Can it happen again?

than ever before in the history of any land." Many people thought his election ensured prosperity for the United States.

Hoover cared deeply about the suffering of the American people and was not the typical Republican; he challenged their laissez-faire attitude in regard to government involvement in business, and instead was proactive by asking business leaders to refrain from laying off workers or cutting wages. In addition, he asked Congress to appropriate money for public-works projects, including his Reconstruction Finance Corporation (RFC), which was a large-scale lending institution aimed at helping banks and industries to recover.

However, by 1932, it was clear that Hoover's policies were not working, and the citizens of the United States were more than ready for a new leader to help the country crawl out of the Great Depression. Franklin D. Roosevelt's New Deal ideas sounded promising and U.S. citizens overwhelmingly elected Roosevelt president, making Hoover the scapegoat for the country's financial woes.

Hoover still continued to serve in various capacities in the government and wrote many articles and books over the years. He died in New York City at the age of 90, on October 20, 1964.

Life before
the Crash

The decade between 1920 and 1929 is often called the Roaring Twenties, New Era, Prosperity Decade, or Jazz Age. It was a time of optimism and hope, and the future looked promising. American culture had made huge strides since the end of the previous century, and rapid changes continued to be made during this decade.

Now, looking back on those years, it is hard to comprehend just how different life was then. There were no televisions or computers. Most people did not own a car. Electricity and indoor plumbing were fairly new developments and were still scarce outside of cities. People relied on themselves, friends, and family both for entertainment and for help in case of an emergency. The extent to which people were "on their own" is hard to imagine, because today there are many social safeguards. If a person loses his or her job today, chances are he or she can collect unemployment insurance, which did not exist in 1930. If an elderly woman has worked during her lifetime, she can now collect a monthly Social Security check, another form of insurance that had not yet been developed in the 1920s. Private relief agencies existed to help out widows and orphans or the elderly poor, but for the most part, families looked after their own.

Americans were proud of their self-sufficiency. Most did not feel the government should play a part in their private lives and were happy that the government felt the same way. The most involvement the majority of people had with the federal government was when they used the postal service to mail a letter.

With the end of World War I in 1918, the country turned back to developing domestically. Many people were intent on enjoying themselves. Jazz music became all the rage, filling smoky clubs and radio airwaves. Its popularity caused writer F. Scott Fitzgerald to call the era the Jazz Age. "The Charleston" was one of the more popular dance crazes sweeping the nation. And women became increasingly "modern," cutting their hair short, wearing baggy dresses that exposed their arms and legs, wearing makeup, and daring to smoke cigarettes in public. These "flappers" fought for social freedoms, while their political counterparts, the suffragettes, rallied to get the right to vote (which they did in 1920, with the passage of the Nineteenth Amendment).

The temperance movement, which worked to make the manufacturing, transportation, and sale of alcohol illegal, began during World War I, and was successful when the Eighteenth Amendment to the Constitution was ratified in 1919. (It was then repealed by the Twenty-First Amendment in 1933.) During the period in which alcohol was illegal, known as Prohibition, many people ignored the law, opening private clubs in homes and the back rooms of stores. Known as "speakeasies," these clubs served alcohol and gained a bad reputation. Many of them were owned by gangsters, and violence became more prevalent. Other people learned to brew their own beer or make gin at home, sometimes in large vats or even in their

The temperance movement, which promoted abstaining from drinking alcohol, led Congress to pass the Eighteenth Amendment to the U.S. Constitution in 1917, which prohibited the manufacture, sale, and consumption of alcoholic beverages in the United States. Then-New York City deputy police commissioner John A. Leach is pictured here watching Prohibition agents dump liquor into a sewer after a raid in 1921.

bathtubs, earning this home-brewed alcohol the name "bathtub gin."

MOVING INTO THE 1920s

Up until the late 1800s, Americans grew or made just about everything they needed to live, buying the few items they could not produce at home. But as the country became increasingly industrialized, Americans began to purchase more household items. Farmers also began to join this "market economy." Instead of raising a variety of livestock and a diversity of crops, they increasingly raised just one crop, sold it, and bought everything else. As farms became more efficient through the development of new machinery for harvesting crops and baling hay, for example, a surplus was created that could be sold elsewhere. During World War I, buyers for those products were found in the war-torn countries of Europe, which were too damaged to produce enough food for their citizens.

Electricity allowed many homes to run such newly invented luxuries as refrigerators, fans, toasters, washing machines, vacuum cleaners, and radios. Suddenly, these became "must-have" items and a shift in the cultural mind-set occurred. Before long, the traditional values of frugality and saving for the future gave way to something new: buying on credit. By 1929, almost 15 percent of all purchases were made on credit. And this "easy way to buy" was encouraged by advertisers, who found their job even easier by promoting their products on the radio.

With all these new gadgets cutting the time spent on housework in half, Americans suddenly had newfound leisure time. Some of them used this free time to take drives in the country in their new cars. Henry Ford's Model T was a car for the masses, and at around $600 to $800, many people could afford one—on credit, of course. Another favorite leisure activity was watching sports games or listening to them on the radio. Baseball and boxing fans listened avidly to broadcasts of their favorite teams and bouts and followed the lives of sports figures, who were the celebrities people most admired. Lou Gehrig and Joe Louis, for example, were seen as heroes for their achievements on the field and in their everyday lives, too. So for many, or even most Americans, the 1920s was a time to live life to the fullest, without much thought of the future.

THE STATE OF THE ECONOMY

Although unemployment was low during the 1920s, wages were also low, and company owners had little incentive to raise them. The bulk of the country's wealth was concentrated in the hands of a few. Six out of 10 families had incomes of less than $2,000 per year and only 3 of every 100 families earned incomes of more than $10,000 a year, the equivalent of about $116,000 in today's dollars. The bottom line was that only a small proportion of the population had the money to make purchases with cash. The increasing debt load on individuals and families worsened the Great Depression, as many consumers simply could not repay their loans. In addition, new technologies meant that factories were able to produce goods faster than consumers were able to purchase them, leaving factories with surplus products. This forced factory owners to lay off workers, because there was no longer a great need to churn out products.

Railroads, factories, mines, and other industries were owned by private individuals who ran their companies in their own ways. There were few, if any, governmental controls over management. Employees often worked long hours for low pay, but as long as there was a steady supply of new immigrants and an influx of young men from rural locations to the cities, all of whom were eager and willing to work for whatever salary and under whatever conditions, the status quo was not about to change.

Some changes had been made in working conditions by President Theodore "Teddy" Roosevelt, who entered office in 1901 after President William McKinley was assasinated. Unfortunately, some of those reforms hurt, rather than helped, certain industries and their employees. For example, as oil became more popular than coal for heating homes, unemployment rose in coal-mining areas such as the Appalachian region. As newly developed synthetic materials replaced cotton in clothing (as well as the fact that styles of the day used less fabric to begin with), the cotton industry suffered. Then there were the farmers, who did not know what to do with their surplus crops. As Europe recovered from the war and its farmers went back to their fields, American farmers lost a valuable market. This loss created a cash shortage, keeping American farmers from buying necessary farm equipment and fertilizer. Planting the same crop year after year in the same field used up the nutrients in the soil, and the weather during this period was uncooperative. Drought followed by floods decimated crops and added to the downward cycle of events.

The federal government may have been able to help farmers recover more quickly from some of their losses, but Calvin Coolidge, the president at the time, told the chairman of the Farm Loan Board, "Farmers have never had money. I don't believe we can do much about it."[1] Coolidge twice vetoed legislation that would have provided relief to farmers and protected them from foreign competition. Most Americans at the time believed in this form of "leave-alone" or "laissez-faire" governing. They believed that their system of government and economy had built-in checks and balances and they did not want the federal government solving their problems or telling them what to do.

So for some, the Great Depression began almost 10 years before it did for the rest of the country. Many farmers could not make their mortgage payments, and banks became overwhelmed by properties they had seized after farmers failed to make their payments. The banks then tried to sell those properties, but no one wanted to buy land to grow crops for which there was not a market. More than 1,500 banks closed between 1926 and 1928 because they had overextended credit.

Economies rise and fall; consequently, this depression was not the first the United States had experienced. In fact, it was the nineteenth depression since the American Revolution. In 1837 and 1857, depressions occurred in the United States due to several factors, including over-speculation in railroads and real estate, an increase in agricultural production, and a shift to more of a manufacturing economy. Again, in 1869, after the gold rush in California, investors raced to buy up gold, and when the supply of gold grew and prices dropped, a panic ensued. The depression of the 1930s, however, was by far the worst.

THE ALLURE OF MONEY

Many people are naturally attracted to making money. Buying and selling stocks was, and often still is, seen as a way of making money quickly and easily. When enough people invest in a certain stock, it can cause the price to rise. If too many people continue to buy and share prices continue to rise, stock prices will eventually become unrealistic in relation to the true value of the company they represent. Unless that true value "catches up" with the stock price, the price will begin to fall. When a share of stock loses value, some people sell their shares, afraid they will lose everything if they do not get rid of the devalued stock. If too many sell too quickly, panic can set in, with investors believing they won't get back at least what they paid for the share. This is what happened in October 1929.

People's overuse of credit soon extended to buying stocks on credit. Known as buying on margin, investors could now buy more stock than they could afford, buoyed by the belief that when the value of their stock rose, they could sell it and pay off their debt. People invested a great deal of their money in such companies as General Motors, DuPont, and RCA (Radio Corporation of America). RCA was just about the most popular stock of the 1920s because of the growing popularity of radio and the company's domination of that market.

Individuals were not the only ones who bought stock for themselves. Banks invested their depositors' money and others formed companies that existed solely to buy up enough stock of other companies to gain control of them. These "holding companies" grew in popularity and there were many of them. "Stock manipulators" sold stocks and bonds and used the income to buy up enough stock in an existing company to

In 1929, Radio Corporation of America (RCA) was the most heavily traded stock on the New York Stock Exchange. The corporation was founded in 1920 and soon held a monopoly over the communications industry, leading to its astronomical stock price of $114 per share in 1929. Here, RCA's mascot, Nipper the Dog, is depicted in an advertisement for Victor phonographs.

control it. Whenever the promoters needed cash, they created another holding company, and so on. After October 29, 1929, there were no more customers who wanted to buy stock with cash. The owners of the holding companies could no longer make payments on the bonds they had sold. Empires that were built during the 1920s in the entertainment, railroad, and utilities industries often fell hard.

One such empire was built by Samuel Insull, an Englishman who had once been inventor Thomas Edison's private secretary. Insull's company, Commonwealth Edison, was billed as "the world's safest investment." He became a millionaire by manipulating stock from his base in Chicago, where he was active politically and socially. Because of his reputation for being trustworthy, many invested in his utility company, which at one point produced nearly one-eighth of all electric power in the country. However, Insull went bankrupt in 1932, taking thousands of people with him.

Herbert Hoover took office as president in 1929, and soon afterward he commissioned a study by some of the most respected sociologists of the time. The statistical study was to be used as a basis to establish "sound national policies" in the United States for the coming years. The resulting document, titled *Recent Social Trends*, was 1,500 pages long and full of all kinds of data about American life. The scientists discovered that the years since 1890 (they used the 1890 national census as their point of reference) had experienced huge social and economic changes, more than in the entire preceding 100 years.

One of the biggest contradictions they found was the difference in standards of living between the country and the city. (The suburbs did not exist yet.) Almost half of the national population was still living in rural areas in 1929, living a lifestyle that had changed little from 100 years before. Immigrants, who had poured into the United States around the turn of the twentieth century, had a huge impact on American life, economically and culturally. But during the 1920s, the government began to pass laws that limited how many new people the country would accept. In 1928, more than 300,000 people immigrated to the United States, but that number dropped to 23,000 by 1932. And during the decade of the Great Depression, from 1930 to 1940, for the first time the number of people who left the country actually exceeded those who arrived.

Contrary to what many believed and how many lived, the ongoing "bull" market—when people are buying stock and prices are rising—could not last forever. Many believed prices would keep climbing indefinitely, but a few small breaks in the rise of prices made others nervous. Some signs of danger that were mostly ignored included the slowdown in the textile, coal, and farming industries and in business overall. Unemployment had grown slightly throughout 1928, and—a real warning sign for many—construction of new homes declined in 1927. When new homes are not being built, there is less need by consumers for new refrigerators, carpets, furniture, and other home supplies. Fewer factory workers were needed to produce the same amount of products because of improved machinery and production methods. Production then had to be reduced because the supply far exceeded the demand. This was followed by worker layoffs, creating a downward spiral. In addition, most people who could afford a car, radio, or refrigerator, or who wanted to buy these items on credit, already had them by 1929.

The stock market crash of 1929 had devastating and long-lasting effects, unlike those depressions that had come before, which passed fairly quickly. The 1929 crash joined other factors in triggering the Great Depression. It was a decade-long period of economic downturn that affected virtually every resident of the United States and spread throughout the world.

The Buildup to Black Tuesday

The upward spiral in stock prices throughout the 1920s slowed somewhat during 1929, although this mild recession (a short-lived, minor economic slowdown) was barely noticed by most investors. There were subtle signs of a weakening economy, including a few small breaks in the rise of stock prices and the slowdown in industry and new home construction. But overall, no one questioned the bull market, including some leading economists and respected bankers who preached optimism.

Gradually, however, the occasional reports that overspeculation was weakening the market grew more frequent. More and more investors became nervous that perhaps prices had become inflated and they might lose money rather than make more. There were some who predicted a messy end. Shortly after he took office in early 1929, Herbert Hoover attempted to curb the buying frenzy by encouraging financial boards in the government to do what they could to slow it down. He even encouraged newspaper editors to warn their readers about the dangers of overspeculation and the inflated prices of stocks. For the most part, Hoover's entreaties were ignored, because no one wanted the "party" of the Roaring Twenties to end.

WHAT CAUSED THE CRASH?

As has been stated, the consensus among economists and historians today is that no single issue caused the stock market crash of October 29, 1929. Rather, a combination of events, natural and man-made, along with governmental policies, improvements in manufacturing, and the rise in buying on credit, all contributed to the market's sudden downturn. Despite hard lessons learned from past market collapses, speculators continued to borrow and buy, driving stock prices higher and higher.

Many New York banks could not keep up with the demand to buy stocks on margin and had to borrow money from other banks. Often, they would borrow money at low interest rates from the Federal Reserve Bank and then turn around and loan it out at a higher interest rate. The Federal Reserve bank system was created by the Federal Reserve Act of 1913 to establish a central bank to strengthen the country's financial system. It is made up of a board of governors and 12 regional Federal Reserve banks around the country, as well as other, smaller banks. Some economic experts feel that at the time of the stock market crash, the Federal Reserve should have loosened restrictions on borrowing money instead of tightening them.

After large gains were made in the market in early September 1929, some economists made positive predictions for the final quarter of the year. One of these fortune-tellers was Irving Fisher, an economics professor at Yale University, who said on October 17 that prices had reached "what looks like a permanently high plateau."[2] Fisher had been respected for his writing and teaching about economic theories and his opinion

Even several months after the stock market crash in October 1929, Yale economics professor Irving Fisher continued to believe that the U.S. economy would recover. Thus, Fisher's theories were largely discredited due to his inaccurate pronouncement that stock prices had reached their plateau just before the crash.

was highly regarded. His mistaken predictions surrounding the market's performance during the days preceding the crash, however, seriously damaged his reputation.

By early October 1929, many utility companies were coming under scrutiny for some of their stock pricing practices. One of these companies, Edison Electric of Boston (which had been cofounded by Samuel Insull before he moved to Chicago), had applied for a stock split, which was denied by the Massachusetts Public Utility Commission. (In a stock split, shareholders are given two shares for every one they presently hold, although the value of the two shares remains the same as the value of the former share.) The *New York Times* reported on October 12 that the

IRVING CLARK FISHER
(1867–1947)

Notable Economist

Irving Fisher was one of the country's leading economists who made his fortune by inventing the Rolodex, known then as the Visible Index Card System. He invested a large amount of his money in stock, and even months into the crash, he continued to reassure investors that the market was secure. Unfortunately, he lost most of his fortune and reputation before the market began to recover in 1932. In 1930, he wrote *The Stock Market Crash and After,* discussing real growth in the manufacturing sector of the country. This may explain his continued investment in stocks and his optimism over the performance of the market. According to one source, what Fisher considered an increase in manufacturing was actually an increase in manufacturing efficiency (how much each worker could produce), due to improvements in technology manufacturing practices.

reason for the denial involved high electricity rates and the need for the company to drop those rates before raising dividends to investors. This decision caused a drop in Boston Electric's stock price and an investigation by the governor of the commonwealth into the company's operating practices. Massachusetts was not the only state experiencing utility company investigations. The governor of New York at the time, Franklin D. Roosevelt, also instituted an investigation into practices among the utility companies of his state. The stock sell-off the following week began in the public utility sector.

For at least five years prior to the crash, the increase in trading on the stock market was also due in part to the habit of buying stocks with borrowed money. Investors were convinced that prices would continue to go up and they would be able to repay their loans with the sale of the inflated stocks. When stock prices began to fall, speculators became worried, selling off as much stock as they could, causing prices to fall even lower. The ripple effect grew stronger with the passing days, weeks, and months. By the millions, people discovered they were less well-off than they had thought. Their wealth had existed only on paper.

THE NEW YORK STOCK EXCHANGE

The New York Stock Exchange (NYSE), the largest stock exchange in the world, was founded in 1792 in the area of Lower Manhattan that is now Wall Street, when a group of 24 brokers (people who buy and sell shares of stock) agreed to deal only with each other. The exchange was formally established in 1817. By the 1920s, the inner sanctum of the NYSE was like another world. Trading began at 10 A.M. and ended at 3 P.M., both times signaled by the banging of a loud gong. Within the massive, 15,000-square-foot room, floors were padded to reduce noise. Seventeen semi-circular trading posts were set up, each handling a different type of stock. Ticker-tape machines recorded current stock prices on huge ribbons of paper as the price reports came in from around the country. The machines were kept under glass and were connected via telegraph to thousands of other stock exchanges and brokers' offices nationwide. For every 100 million shares traded, 500 miles of tape swirled through the machines.

Stock transactions, including sale prices, were tracked telegraphically through these machines. Today, giant digital readouts announce the latest prices as quickly as transactions are made. In the 1920s, the tickers spewed out printed numbers that were then transcribed onto chalkboards. These tickers were relatively slow, and if transactions took place too rapidly, the tracking mechanisms would fall behind. On Monday, October 21, 1929, the week before the big crash, the ticker ran a full 100 minutes behind actual sales by the end of the day. That delay worsened during the following week. When the ticker fell behind, people were not aware of the actual price of any given stock, and they were not aware of just how much they had lost. Those who tried to get information by phone were equally frustrated, because phone lines were continuously jammed. Lack of adequate communication likely played a large role in the severity of the panic.

THE STOCK MARKET CRAZE

Most experts and investors alike believed that rising stock prices reflected a healthy economy. The government had no policies in place to regulate the market, although the Federal Reserve Board did try to keep investments in balance by occasionally raising interest rates to discourage rampant borrowing. People would think twice before borrowing money, because higher interest rates meant that the borrower would have to pay back much more money than he/she borrowed. In fact, that February, the Federal Bank of New York raised interest rates by one point, from 5 to 6 percent, to discourage "reckless behavior" by speculators who continued to borrow.

The following month, the Federal Reserve Board met secretly, leading to rumors that interest rates would be raised again; consequently, investors began to sell. Rising interest rates

Although the New York Stock Exchange traces its roots back to 1792, its current name was not adopted until 1863. The current home of the New York Stock Exchange, which is pictured here in 1921, opened in 1903 and was designed by American architect George B. Post.

are often believed to have a braking effect on the economy. Stock values are tracked each day by the industrial average—the average value of the price of the top 30 companies trading in the stock exchange. This average is a good indicator of the market's overall performance. One point equals $1.

Charles E. Mitchell, president of the country's largest bank, National City Bank, promised to keep interest rates low and to continue to lend money. The Federal Reserve Board and some of the more influential bankers could have requested congressional approval to set limits on buying on margin, but none of these men wanted to be associated with having ended the boom.

By 1929, it seemed as though everyone, in all walks of life, and not just businessmen, was interested in the stock market. People took out second mortgages on their homes and housewives sneaked money from household expenses to play the market.

CHARLES E. MITCHELL
(1877–1955)

Chairman of the National City Organization

Charles Mitchell served as president of the National City Bank, the nation's largest bank, from 1921 until the market crashed in 1929. He was called a hero during the "mini crash" of March 26, 1929, when he vowed to keep interest rates low, no matter what, and to continue to lend money. Before joining National City, he was an assistant to the president of Western Electric in Chicago and then held the same position at the Trust Company of America in New York City. He was elected president of National City in 1921 but resigned in 1929 to become chairman of the National City Organization, a position he held until 1933. Under his leadership, the bank became a global corporation with 100 offices in 23 countries. He introduced the personal consumer loan in 1928.

Just before the crash, he had borrowed millions of dollars to buy more stock in his own company, trying to stabilize the price of its shares, which had fallen from $500 to $200. He admitted speculating with the bank's stock and was subsequently investigated by federal authorities. He resigned in 1933 and the investigation into his illicit actions led Congress to pass the Securities Act of 1933 and the Banking Acts of 1933 and 1935, which ultimately ended commercial bank ownership of investment firms.

Some people invested everything they had in the market in the belief that there was no way they could *not* become rich.

Investment trusts, which were relatively new at the time, raised investors' confidence even more. These trusts combined stocks of many companies in one grouping, so buying shares in an investment trust actually meant purchasing stock in many different companies. Because these funds were managed by professional financial advisors and were diversified (made up of a variety of companies), people felt more secure buying stock this way. Using a professional took the guesswork out of investing. High levels of speculation in some stocks pushed prices well above what companies were actually worth. Most investors did not worry about these inflated prices, however, believing that they represented the future worth of the companies—the companies' potential, not the present reality. Unfortunately, diversification of stocks within a trust or fund did not help investors at the time of the crash because of the universal drop in prices in all categories.

HEADING TOWARD A CRASH

Stock prices reached their high point on September 3, 1929. Two days later, economist Roger Babson said in a speech to the National Business Conference, "Sooner or later a crash is coming and it may be terrific. Factories will shut down and men will be thrown out of work. The vicious circle will get in full swing and the result will be a serious business depression." The industrial average dropped as the market responded to his prediction, but it recovered the next day. This dip became known as the Babson Break.[3] He was one of the few who accurately predicted the coming crash publicly.

Fewer new homes were constructed during the fall, adding to lower production across all industries, which caused the recession to deepen. On October 19, more than 3 million shares were traded and the industrial average fell yet again. Five days later, on October 24 (often called Black Thursday), the industrial average fell to that previous June's level, erasing any profits stockholders

On October 24, 1929, in an effort to stem the tide of dropping stock prices, then-NYSE vice president Richard Whitney was asked by several prominent Wall Street bankers to purchase stock shares of major U.S. corporations at higher prices. Unfortunately, Whitney's efforts only served to delay the crash, which would occur five days later on October 29.

had made in the four months in between. The heavy trading and fall of the industrial average caused the day to begin on a sour note at the New York Stock Exchange, with General Motors' company stock selling well below its previous market price.

Throughout that day, Richard Whitney, vice president of the NYSE, placed buy orders at each trading station on the floor of the exchange. And at noon, top bankers set up a $50 million fund in the hope of bolstering falling stock prices. These measures helped restore some calm and order, and the market closed 12 points down from the day before. In total, 12,894,650 shares were traded on Black Thursday, a new record. The previous record for trading activity had been set about 18 months before, on March 12, 1928, when 3,875,910 shares were traded. On the day after Black Thursday, a *New York Times* headline stated, "Worst Stock Crash Stemmed by Banks: 12,894,650-share Day Swamps Market: Leaders Confer, Find Conditions Sound."[4]

That Friday and Saturday, October 25 and 26, trading remained heavy, but prices were fairly steady. In 1929, the stock market was open for trading six days a week. But Sunday, October 27, 1929, was no normal day off for those who worked there. From bankers and brokers to clerks, offices were full of people trying to recover from the never-before experienced highs and lows of the week before. It seemed that all of New York was reacting to the unprecedented events of that day. Restaurants normally closed on Sundays opened their doors for tourists who flocked to the district to see for themselves where all the excitement had taken place; perhaps some wanted to take home souvenirs of the ticker tape that littered the streets.

Monday's opening gong started a selling frenzy and the industrial average fell 38 points that day, representing the largest drop in prices ever. The bankers did not rescue investors this time. In fact, that evening, they released a statement saying their goal was to maintain order within the market, not to protect anyone's profit or keep prices at a certain level. Everyone was preparing for what might happen the next day.

The Day
of the Crash

In New York City, Black Tuesday, October 29, 1929, dawned cloudy, as if nature had anticipated the coming events. With trading expected to be heavy, extra brokers, switchboard operators, and clerks were brought in. Every type of business that traded on the market was privy to the rampant selling of stocks. In the first half hour, 3.5 million shares traded hands. This was the day the large investors—the millionaires—sold in a panic; small investors had already lost everything the previous week. Huge losses were experienced by nearly everyone. For example, RCA shares were selling for $26, down from a high of $114 (adjusted to the 5 to 1 stock split earlier that year). The ticker quickly fell behind and it soon became impossible to tell how the market was really doing or to find out the latest sale price. News and rumors spread quickly.

SELL, SELL, SELL

By early afternoon, five top bankers decided to set up a meeting. They were Charles Mitchell, chairman of National City Bank; Albert Wiggin, chairman of Chase National Bank; William Potter, president of Guaranty Trust Company; Seward Prosser, chairman of Bankers Trust Company; and Thomas W. Lamont, senior partner of J.P. Morgan & Company. After the meeting, Lamont made the following statement to reporters: "There has been a little distress selling on the Stock Exchange, and we have held a meeting of the heads of several financial institutions to discuss the situation. We have found that there are no houses in difficulty and reports from brokers indicate that margins are being maintained satisfactorily. . . . It is the consensus of the group that many of the quotations on the Stock Exchange did not fairly represent the situation."[5]

His statement was not totally true, because brokers struggled to keep up with the flood of sell orders. The volume was unprecedented and the floor of the exchange was in chaos. Adding to the confusion were the customers who had been unable to get through on the telephone and came to the exchange in person to try to get information. Their presence did little to help the growing pandemonium, and it was nearly impossible for them to get any additional accurate and up-to-date information anyway. Everyone was operating more or less in the dark.

Word spread that prominent financiers such as William C. Durant and the Rockefeller family were stepping in, and people stopped telling brokers to sell, hoping the market would once again bounce back. The strategy worked for a little while, but sell orders continued coming in from other parts of the country that were not aware of the financiers' strategy. Panic began to build again. Telegrams from brokers to speculators (who had bought on margin) overwhelmed the Western Union system with terse messages: Cover your margin now, or your shares will be sold when the market reopens. Investors and their brokers were reduced to tears.

RICHARD WHITNEY
(1888–1974)

President of the
New York Stock Exchange

Richard Whitney came from a wealthy Boston, Massachusetts, family and attended Harvard University. When he moved to New York City in 1910, he opened a bond brokerage firm—Richard Whitney and Company—with his brother. Two years later, the company bought a seat on the New York Stock Exchange (NYSE). Whitney moved among the powerful socialites of the city and gained power and prestige. In 1919, he was elected to the board of governors of the stock exchange and shortly thereafter, he became vice president of NYSE. On Black Thursday, October 24, 1929, several prominent Wall Street bankers met in an attempt to stop the market slide. They jointly agreed to have Whitney attempt to end the slide by having him purchase large amounts of stock shares in prominent U.S. corporations, such as U.S. Steel, at rates much higher than market value. Unfortunately, Whitney's actions only stemmed the tide of the impending crash, and by the following Tuesday, the market bottomed out. During this tumultuous period, Whitney served as acting head of NYSE, but was elevated to president by the exchange's board of governors in 1930 and soon thereafter began advising President Herbert Hoover.

Unfortunately for Whitney, his popularity would not last much longer. Although many thought he was a brilliant financier, in reality, he had borrowed a lot of money before and after the crash from his brother and his wealthy friends. After he could no longer obtain loans, he resorted to embezzling funds from the NYSE Gratuity Fund and the New York Yacht Club, where he was treasurer. He also stole $800,000 in bonds from his father-in-law's estate. On March 10, 1938, he was charged with embezzlement, and served three years in prison.

Once the stock market crash began on October 29, many stockholders crowded the streets outside the New York Stock Exchange when they were unable to contact their brokers. As rumors of the crash began to spread, mounted policemen were brought in to control the crowd.

Thousands gathered on Wall Street that afternoon, as rumors of a crash began to spread. Police on horseback were brought in to keep the crowd under control. By 3 P.M., the industrial average had dropped to 230, down an additional 43 points from the day before. This represented a loss of about 12 percent for the day—a total of nearly 40 percent from its high of September 3, less than two months before. It was now at the same level as it had been in November 1928. More than $14 billion was lost in the 16,410,030 shares that had been traded—

a new record. The entire budget of the U.S. federal government in 1929 was just $3 billion.

The next day, investors sold 16 million shares even though it meant losing money. The atmosphere on Black Tuesday and the days immediately following was one of panic. Investors, brokers, bankers—everyone was panicked. This was worse than the selling frenzies that had happened in the past. This was a sustained, prolonged period of such frenzy that panic gripped all those involved.

A DOWNWARD SPIRAL

The next few days of trading created a mess of the traders' records. By the following Wednesday, the NYSE Board of Governors voted to close the exchange for two days to give everyone a chance to catch up. This was the first time the stock exchange had been closed since the start of World War I in 1914. Records were straightened out, but the sell-off continued when the market reopened the following Monday, and trading was subsequently limited to three hours a day. There were some who tried to maintain an optimistic outlook, and in spite of the obvious problems, some financial writers wrote that the economy was still strong. President Hoover even stated that "the fundamental business of the country, that is, production and distribution of commodities, is on a sound and prosperous basis."[6]

But no matter how strong the reassurances, the market continued its gradual downward spiral throughout the next two months. By mid-November, activity on Wall Street had slowed. People found it nearly impossible to believe that $30 billion in paper value was gone. Wall Street's credibility had declined and the U.S. credit system had been badly damaged. It wasn't long before unemployment began to rise. The market finally hit bottom in July 1932, when the industrial average was down slightly more than 89 percent from its high in mid-1929.

Even the savviest financial experts could not have predicted the depths to which the U.S. economy would fall, and the drastic, tragic effects it would have on the country's social fabric. By the height of the Great Depression, the national income was cut in half and 75 percent of all stock market values had disappeared. By the time Franklin Roosevelt took office in 1933, 25 percent of all workers were out of work. Today, unemployment is considered "unacceptable" when it reaches about 5 percent.

THE EFFECT OF THE CRASH

With the loss of employment, families quickly found themselves in financial trouble. They had trouble feeding themselves and paying rent and utilities. For the most part, savings were nonexistent. Much of the country's savings had been spent on stock speculation over the course of the past decade. Families sold furniture, jewelry, and anything else of value. For those in the cities who rented apartments, missing a rent payment often meant immediate eviction. Homelessness, especially in the cities, very quickly became a major problem. Social service agencies that had always been around to provide for the poor were quickly overwhelmed by requests for aid. Those who owned their homes were sometimes able to work out deals with their banks, because the banks had nothing to gain by seizing the home. After all, whom would they get to buy it? In some cases, families would send children to live with various relatives so the parents would be free to move around in search of work.

Some companies tried to reinvigorate failing business by cutting prices. The Ford Motor Company, for example, dropped prices on all its car models, which came out to be about $500 for the standard car—still an astronomical sum for most. Comedians found dark humor in the situation and joked that people should carry open umbrellas when walking around New York City to protect themselves from the rain of investors jumping from rooftops and windows in despair over lost fortunes.

Certain segments of the population had always had a difficult time getting by, but the middle class really felt the losses this time. There was no sense of security for these shopkeepers, managers, lawyers, accountants, and other professionals. Many teachers lost their jobs, causing schools to close; but those teachers who kept their jobs often went unpaid or were paid just a portion of their former salary. Still, some teachers helped provide food for their hungry students, knowing that whatever they ate at school might be their only meal of the day.

All told, about 3 million Americans were directly affected by the events of October 29, 1929, and the aftermath. Those who had borrowed money to buy stock, furniture, jewelry, homes, and cars had their belongings repossessed. Many people went bankrupt. Lives were unalterably changed. Some people even took their own lives when they realized the enormity of what had happened to them.

HOOVER'S SOLUTION

Early in the Great Depression, the federal government, led by President Hoover and other conservatives, believed that the best solution was for Americans to continue to rely on themselves. It was believed that a continued effort at self-reliance would help the people "pull themselves up by their bootstraps." The prevailing belief was that the marketplace would adjust itself eventually and the government should not intervene. This method of "laissez-faire" governing was all Americans had ever known, and at first, most people did try to care for themselves and their families without reaching out to social service agencies for help.

By the time some families did ask for help, they had lost almost everything they owned, including the roof over their heads. State and local relief agencies, originally established to help widows and orphans, were overwhelmed with requests for money and food. The timing of the crash was especially difficult, because winter was right around the corner. Furniture

During the early part of the Great Depression, many Republicans believed that the government should refrain from getting involved in people's lives. Instead, they believed that American citizens, such as these New York City street vendors, should "pull themselves up by their bootstraps."

was burned for heat and two meals a day became standard for many.

Hoover felt that government aid would ultimately weaken Americans' character and would undermine one of the guiding principles of the country. A statement made by the president in February 1931 underscored his philosophy:

> This is not an issue as to whether people shall go hungry or cold in the United States. It is solely a question of the best method by which hunger and cold shall be prevented. It is a

question of whether the American people . . . will maintain the spirit of charity and mutual self-help. If we break down this sense of responsibility and individual generosity in times of national difficulty and if we start appropriations of this character, we have impaired something infinitely valuable in the life of the American people. I am confident that our people have the resources, the initiative, the courage, the stamina, and the kindliness of spirit to meet this situation in the way they have met their problems over generations.[7]

Hoover's administration was not immune to the peoples' suffering. But its beliefs were so ingrained, it could see no other way to move out of the depression while maintaining America's hallmark reliance on self. Hoover did not just sit by and do nothing. Efforts were made to slow the effects of the crash. In 1932, Hoover established the Reconstruction Finance Corporation (RFC) to loan money to state and local governments, which would use it to start public works projects, and to failing businesses, including banks, railroads, insurance companies, and farm mortgage organizations. He felt that if these businesses were able to remain solvent, they would continue to employ workers. The RFC eventually loaned out about $2 billion.

One of the most well-known projects the RFC helped fund was the building of Hayden Planetarium in New York City's Central Park, with a $650,000 loan from the RFC and a $150,000 donation from philanthropist Charles Hayden. The planetarium opened in 1935. Other high-profile projects included the building of Jones Beach in New York, the Bay Bridge in San Francisco, and the Pennsylvania Turnpike. But as the only program set up to help deal with the crisis on a national level, the RFC was not enough.

To bolster Hoover's attempts, some private individuals tried their own tactics to reinvigorate the economy. Philip H. Gadsden, president of the Philadelphia Chamber of Commerce, started a "Buy Now" campaign, urging everyone who had a job to go out and spend just 15 cents a day. He claimed that if every wage earner in the country would do this every day, it would free up enough money to create jobs for millions of the unemployed and pay them $6.25 per day. He said this contribution would put more than $2 million back into circulation each year. Launched in November 1930, it initially seemed like a success, with copycat campaigns springing up throughout the country. However, it fizzled out almost as quickly, because people did not really have that much money to spend every day. It seems odd today that 15 cents would put a strain on a family's budget, but it did.

Other fund-raising efforts were undertaken to fill the coffers of social service organizations. One effort was to take the money received during certain shows at movie theaters and donate it to specific agencies. In addition, President Hoover set up a group known as the Committee on Mobilization of Relief Resources of the President's Organization for Unemployment Relief. Headed by Owen D. Young, chairman of General Electric, this group used billboards and magazine and newspaper ads to remind Americans they were in the middle of a depression (as if they needed reminding), and that millions of fellow citizens needed assistance.

New York City held various fund-raising events, including dinner dances for the wealthy, basketball games, carnivals, concerts, and movies, and even a door-to-door fund drive that asked for donations of a onetime minimum payment of $2 or a dime a week. More than $1 million was raised through these efforts, but private organizations eventually ran out of money, too. Although these various campaigns were admirable, and people did reach out to help their neighbors, what was needed was massive relief on a scale the country had never known. But people needed more than charity. They wanted to earn real wages, and that was an issue that was not addressed in Hoover's approach to ending the Great Depression. As the depression deepened, and people's support of the federal government's approach lessened, the time was ripe for a change in leadership.

The Early Years
of the Great
Depression

A common Great Depression-era image is of men standing on street corners selling apples. These small businesses were made possible by the International Apple Shippers Association, which came up with the following slogan to sell its surplus fruit: "Buy an apple a day and send the Depression away!" Apples were selling for a nickel each, and at the program's height, there were about 20,000 apple stands operating in New York City alone. Another novel business tactic was tandem shoe shiners. One would stand on the sidewalk and call attention to a man's scuffed shoes, while his helper waited nearby with a rag and shoeshine kit. Other ventures were attempted, including a real long shot: In Colorado in 1932, thousands took an eight-day course offered by the state Vocational Training Board in panning for gold!

UNEMPLOYMENT BECOMES RAMPANT

As unemployment rates climbed, wages dropped. Sales clerks in stores might earn $5 a week. Factory workers made 25 cents an hour. Secretaries worked for $10 a week and house servants only $10 a month. In cities, hundreds would line up for jobs in factories or on the docks, where only a handful of workers were needed.

As men lost their jobs and days of unemployment stretched into months, the prevailing view of men as heads of their households, provider and protector, was damaged. The men who could no longer provide for their families were often frustrated and confused about what to do and how to conduct themselves. Women, as a result, often took on more leadership roles. This role reversal played havoc with the traditional family. As more men lost their jobs, working women, especially married working women, were often thought to be taking work away from men.

In reality, the jobs that women held were for the most part jobs men would not want anyway. Women's work was generally domestic or as teachers and office workers and nurses. They rarely worked in industry or semiskilled labor such as the jobs men tended to have. Women also made substantially less money than men. There were those who called for all working women to be fired and replaced by unemployed men. Some said there were about the same number of employed women as unemployed men, so they could easily replace each other. This argument was strenuously objected to by women's organizations, including the National Federation of Business and Professional Women's Clubs, which called this attack on working women the most serious problem since women fought for the right to vote.

Others made the argument that a woman's place was in the home, where she was responsible to take care of her husband, children, and running the household. They claimed that there was a direct relationship between the increase in women in the workplace and the falling birthrate. However, during the Great Depression, these arguments were unsupportable, because most women worked to provide for their families, not out of a desire for a career, according to the Women's Bureau of the Department of Labor. The bureau went on to state that

ELEANOR ROOSEVELT
(1884–1962)

Advocate for Social Change

On October 11, 1884, Eleanor Roosevelt was born into New York's prominent and wealthy Roosevelt family. Eleanor was the niece of Theodore Roosevelt, the twenty-sixth president of the United States, and would later marry her fifth cousin, Franklin. Eleanor had a rough childhood; she was shy and withdrawn and had a mother who openly rejected her. Her mother died when she was eight, and at age 10, she lost her father, with whom she was very close. She and Franklin married on March 17, 1905, and within 11 years, she had six children. (One son died as a baby.)

From the beginning, Eleanor helped Franklin in the political realm. She was a unique First Lady, taking an active role in the country's affairs, and acting almost as an assistant president. She traveled around the country investigating results of New Deal policies and speaking on behalf of the poor and unemployed, while also denigrating racial inequality. She spoke often on radio and wrote a newspaper column titled "My Day." Her willingness to speak her mind openly earned her friends as well as enemies. For example, her support of women's rights was one cause that earned her both. She openly advocated for an increased role for women in society.

After Franklin's death in 1945, she served as a spokeswoman for the United Nations until her death in 1962.

competition in the workplace was not usually between men and women, because few jobs held by women could be transferred to men.

Eleanor Roosevelt wrote in the September 1939 issue of *Current History and Forum:*

> Many women, after marriage, find plenty of work in the home. They have no time, no inclination or no ability for any other kind of work. The records show that very few married women work from choice, that they are working only because a husband is ill or had deserted them, or there are special expenses caused by illness or educational requirements in the home. There may even be fathers, mothers, sisters, or brothers to be supported. It seems to me that it is far more important for us to think about creating more jobs than it is for us to worry about how we are going to keep any groups from seeking work.[8]

STRIKING OUT ON THEIR OWN

Men who could not find work and could no longer support their families sometimes left their loved ones behind to search for a job. A large subculture grew around the country, consisting of just such men. They would follow the routes of the railroads, hopping freight cars to get from one town to the next. Jumping on trains was dangerous, and more than one man ended up dead under the wheels of a train. Also, food and jobs were scarce everywhere, so no matter where he hopped off, a man was unlikely to be much better off than he had been before. Families routinely had many children, and it became nearly impossible to feed and clothe them all, so sometimes the eldest son was sent out to fend for himself. Decisions were made to allow the teen boys in the family to head out on their own, just as their fathers were doing.

These men and boys—and only occasionally women and girls, who might disguise themselves as men to avoid being harassed—formed little communities of "hobos" around

Throughout the United States, food and jobs were scarce during the Great Depression. Here, a group of jobless and homeless men wait in line to get a free meal at New York City's Municipal Lodging House during the winter of 1932–33.

railroad yards and on the outskirts of towns. They shared a common fire to cook whatever food they had scavenged or begged for and shared a common desire to find a job and return to a life of normalcy. Sometimes they formed a kind of family and worked together to earn what money they could, and shared what they were able to buy with it. Sometimes these travelers were welcomed by kind strangers who ran soup kitchens or missions like the Salvation Army; but more often, they were chased off the trains by conductors and out of the towns by the local police.

Soon, slums called shantytowns sprang up on the fringes of cities. Huts and shacks were built from whatever materials were available: scraps of wood, boxes, crates, tin, and cardboard. These ramshackle villages were dubbed "Hoovervilles" after the president whose policies many grew to hate. Herbert Hoover's popularity began to wane within months after the crash, because he failed to establish massive relief programs to aid the unemployed. He was steadfast in his belief in the individual's ability to recover from any disaster, but his seeming indifference caused mass resentment.

Life was difficult in the hobo communities and Hoovervilles. Sanitation was poor, and fresh water was difficult to obtain. Disease was prevalent, and despair often led to violence, making these men even less welcome in the areas they lived. They found what work they could, laboring as migrant workers or doing construction jobs or other manual tasks. The Hoovervilles often were built near city dumps. Men and boys routinely scavenged for food, usable clothing, or other objects that other people had thrown away.

In some cases, families were literally starving. It was difficult to get fresh vegetables, proteins, or milk. Parents went without food so their children could eat. The meager meals often consisted of coffee, bread with or without butter, sometimes potatoes or rice, and leftovers received from local markets. People in the country lived off the land, picking berries and wild vegetables. Many people survived by receiving meager relief checks that might be as little as $4 to $5 per week for a whole family. Sometimes families were given vouchers

The Great Depression affected some Americans more than others. For instance, some unemployed people were forced to sell their houses and move to "Hoovervilles," where they had to live in squalid conditions. Pictured here is a Hooverville in Seattle, Washington, where unemployment reached 26 percent by January 1935.

with a list of what foods they were allowed to "purchase" and in what quantities.

DIFFERENT EXPERIENCES

Although the Great Depression affected everyone, it affected everyone differently. Class differences and ethnic and cultural differences equated to different experiences. Many ethnic groups had always experienced suffering from lack of material goods, food, and money. They often were the last hired and the first fired, and they were often the first blamed when something went wrong. Immigrants tended to cluster in groups when arriving in the United States. Often they remained within a short distance of the port where they first landed. Others pushed inland to join already-established enclaves of their countrymen. Their populations were often disproportionately affected by the Great Depression. For example, during the 1930s, blacks made up 17 percent of the population in Baltimore, Maryland, but 32 percent of the unemployed.

Among the various ethnicities populating the United States during the Great Depression, the Native American population was the poorest. In 1934, the U.S. government passed the Wheeler-Howard Act, which gave to all tribes the right to decide if they would accept new privileges in education, self-government, and economic independence. Part of Roosevelt's Works Progress Administration (WPA) encouraged a renewed interest in folk culture, including that of Native Americans. These encouragements helped save some of the traditional ways of the tribes, whose members had previously endured efforts by the government to eradicate the old ways in favor of white ways.

Filipinos were another group deeply affected by the Great Depression. When the United States took the Philippines from Spain after the Spanish–American War in 1898, Filipinos became "naturalized," but did not become American citizens. They were allowed to enter the United States freely, and by the time of the crash, nearly 45,000 had settled in the country, mostly in California. They worked mainly on the farms there, harvesting spinach, strawberries, and other crops. Some moved north to pick beets in Montana, potatoes in Idaho, and apples in Washington.

At the beginning of the Great Depression, 3 million Mexicans called the United States home. Many had migrated north as laborers, lured with the promise of making more money. Eventually, about half of them returned to their homeland when the depression worsened and the promises did not come true. And although many *chose* to return to Mexico, hundreds of thousands were "repatriated" by the U.S. government in order to open up jobs for "real" Americans.

In the South, small inroads were made against segregation, as blacks and whites often joined to help impoverished families, friends, and neighbors. As groups protested unfair hiring practices in the early 1930s, a popular slogan became "Black and white, unite and fight!"[9] Unions were also formed to help southern farmworkers. The Share Croppers Union was one that began in 1931 and by 1934 had 8,000 members, including some whites. But farmwork became increasingly mechanized; there was less of a need for workers to pick crops by hand, and unions became less useful and eventually disbanded.

World War I veterans of all ethnicities joined in 1932 in a march on Washington, D.C., to demand payment of a bonus that had been promised by the government but never received. Immigrants and descendants of slaves joined white veterans appealing for their money. The tent city that sprang up in Washington housed men of all colors; the men worked, ate, and slept side by side. President Hoover, however, had no patience for the vets and authorized the U.S. Army to drive them from the capital, which they did using tear gas and bayonets.

A CHANGE IN LEADERSHIP

The American people's support for President Hoover did not last through the presidential election of 1932. When the Great Depression began, he approached various businesses and tried to talk them into taking lower profits, and asked them not to cut pay or lay people off. But he avoided direct orders to get business owners to comply with his requests. He wanted everyone—business owners, unions, and workers—to volunteer in making sacrifices. He believed in a trickle-down theory: If he could help revive the banks and businesses, then the benefits would trickle down to the workers.

Although he urged Congress to create public works programs and attempted to convince state and local governments to help private charities care for destitute Americans, President Herbert Hoover refrained from directly involving the U.S. government in the affairs of its citizens. Hoover is pictured here shortly before the presidential election of 1932, when he was defeated by Franklin D. Roosevelt.

But Americans were ready for a more drastic change. That change came in the form of a former state governor and Democrat, Franklin Delano Roosevelt. He was elected governor of New York in 1928, serving when Hoover was the president. Roosevelt campaigned for president in 1932 on the platform that the depth of the crisis facing the country demanded that the government should help solve the problem. He said in a campaign speech, "I pledge you, I pledge myself, to a new deal for the American people." The phrase "new deal" was picked up by a reporter, reprinted, and came to represent all the programs proposed by Roosevelt while in office. His supporters and fellow advocates of these programs became known as "New Dealers."

During the campaign, conservative Republicans wanted to follow the country's current course, which was to keep

FRANKLIN DELANO ROOSEVELT
(1882–1945)

Leader of a Nation in Distress

Franklin Delano Roosevelt was born into a wealthy family in 1882 in Hyde Park, New York. He graduated from Harvard University and Columbia Law School. He entered politics and was determined to follow in the footsteps of his distant cousin Theodore "Teddy" Roosevelt, the twenty-sixth president of the United States. He married another of his cousins, Eleanor, in 1905. She was independent and outspoken and encouraged her husband's support of the workingman and minorities.

In 1910, Roosevelt began to serve the first of two terms in the U.S. Senate, and in 1913, President Woodrow Wilson appointed Roosevelt assistant secretary of the U.S. Navy. (Interestingly, this was a position his cousin Teddy had also held prior to being elected president.)

In 1921, at the age of 39, Roosevelt was stricken with polio and lost the use of his legs. Determined to walk again, he began a rigorous regimen of physical therapy, especially swimming. Despite his hard work, he never fully recovered. Polio left him unable to walk on his own and he spent most of his time in a wheelchair. Much of the public never knew he was paralyzed, though, even after he became president. He avoided being photographed in his wheelchair in order to maintain an image of strength in an era when those with handicaps were seen as weak. His later compassion and understanding for the unfortunate may have been instilled in him during his struggle with polio.

the government from interfering in people's lives. The liberal Democrats, on the other hand, wanted the U.S. government to nationalize many industries—such as steel, oil, banking, and the railroads—and take over their management. Roosevelt took the middle ground. He proposed a three-pronged solution to the depression: relief, recovery, and reform. Relief was simply immediate aid to those who had been affected the most. Recovery measures were meant to strengthen the economy, and reform programs were intended to be permanent measures in both government and social services.

Roosevelt seemed to have the right ideas at the right time. When he entered office, stock prices were at 11 percent of precrash rates. The suicide rate had risen. Three-quarters of the states had closed banks. More than 9,000 banks had failed. Because this was before the government provided insurance on bank deposits, many Americans lost all their savings. Some schools had closed, and businesses were failing every day. The nation collectively pinned their hopes on one man: Franklin Roosevelt. His enthusiasm, optimism, and charm had endeared him to millions of voters and they came out in droves to support him.

Roosevelt's First 100 Days

President Franklin Roosevelt and his proposals for ending the Great Depression had grown so popular by election day that he won by an overwhelming margin—42 out of 48 states. In a nutshell, Herbert Hoover was viewed as being inflexible and rigid in his beliefs, and Roosevelt was seen as willing to experiment with fresh ideas that might turn the tide of the depression. The crisis had nearly reached its worst point by the time Roosevelt took office in 1933. He wasted no time instituting his policies, and within his first three months in office, known as the First 100 Days, an unprecedented amount of legislation was passed.

FIRESIDE CHATS

Roosevelt was the first president to take full opportunity of the newest mass medium: radio. Like John F. Kennedy, 30 years later, whose magnetism transfixed millions on television, Roosevelt exuded confidence that inspired just about everyone who heard him. In his inaugural address given on March 4, 1933, he spoke in his characteristic, straightforward style, getting to the core of the country's problems: "This is a day of national consecration, and I am certain that my fellow Americans expect that . . . I will address them with a candor which the present situation of our nation impels. This is pre-eminently the time to speak the truth, the whole truth, frankly, and boldly." And then he spoke the line that has become famous: "The only thing we have to fear is fear itself—nameless, unreasoning, unjustified terror which paralyzes needed efforts to convert retreat into advance."

He continued:

> We must act, and act quickly . . . if we are to go forward, we must move as a trained and loyal army willing to sacrifice for the good of a common discipline, because without such discipline, no progress is made, no leadership becomes effective. I am prepared under my constitutional duty to recommend the measures that a stricken nation in the midst of a stricken world may require. I shall wage a war against the emergency as great as the power that would be given to me if we were in fact invaded by a foreign foe.[10]

He added that the nation would endure, revive, and prosper, and he promised to demand broad executive powers to meet his goals if Congress did not do the job. He planned to attack on several fronts, using direct government intervention to create jobs, rebuild business, provide relief, and institute wide-ranging reforms. Because government involvement in Americans' private lives had been virtually nonexistent up until this time, some persuasion was necessary for the people to accept what Roosevelt was proposing. But his timing was perfect. After more than three years of a strangling depression, the people were ready for a change. Roosevelt knew his first three months in office were the crucial time to put actions behind his words. This First 100 Days

After he was elected president, Franklin D. Roosevelt wasted little time in reaching out to the American people. Roosevelt is pictured here during his first radio address at his New York City townhouse on November 9, 1932, with his mother, Sara Delano Roosevelt (seated at left), his son James, and his daughter Anna Roosevelt Dall.

became famous for the sheer volume of legislation he was able to put in place. The support he received in Congress was almost universal, and bills were passed at an unprecedented pace.

Just as he had used radio to campaign for office and to broadcast his inaugural address, he now used the medium to become a part of Americans' lives on an ongoing basis. His weekly radio addresses became known as "fireside chats," and people tuned in eagerly to listen to their president. He used radio to encourage (or, his opponents claimed, to brainwash)

FIRESIDE CHATS

President Franklin D. Roosevelt fully understood the importance of reaching out to Americans in a manner of a friend or kindly uncle. He adopted the practice of weekly radio addresses that made listeners feel so comfortable with their president, as if he were actually sitting with them in their living rooms. His words were directed at each listener, without the filter of a newspaper reporter. These talks came to be called "fireside chats." The first such address was given on March 12, 1933, in which the president explained why he had closed the banks and what he hoped to accomplish by doing so:

> I want to talk for a few minutes with the people of the United States about banking—with the comparatively few who understand the mechanics of banking but more particularly with the overwhelming majority who use banks for the making of deposits and the drawing of checks. I want to tell you what has been done in the last few days, why it was done, and what the next steps are going to be. I recognize that the many proclamations from state capitols and from Washington, the legislation, the treasury regulations, etc., couched for the most part in banking and legal terms, should be explained for the benefit of the average citizen. I owe this in particular because of the fortitude and good temper with which everybody has accepted the inconvenience and hardships of the banking holiday. I know that when you understand what we in Washington have been about, I shall continue to have your cooperation as fully as I have had your sympathy and help during the past week.

and enlighten all Americans. He became a familiar part of their lives, so familiar that people felt they knew him intimately. It often seemed as if Roosevelt was sitting across the parlor discussing world affairs face-to-face.

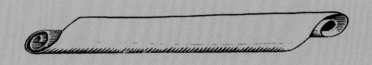

Roosevelt went on to explain how banks invest their customers' deposits; that the money does not just sit in a vault waiting to be withdrawn. He told listeners that banks put their money to work, investing it in various forms of bonds and loans, and that only a small fraction of all deposits are actually available for withdrawal as cash at any given time. He repeated that people should not hoard their money once the banks reopened and reminded them that it was safer to keep their money in the bank than under their mattresses.

According to historian Robert S. McElvaine, Roosevelt's explanations were so successful that "many of the same people who had rushed to withdraw their funds from banks in the closing days of the Hoover Administration went back as the banks reopened and deposited their money once more."[*] Due to his honesty, Roosevelt gained the trust of the American public. He closed his first chat by saying:

> There is an element in the readjustment of our financial system more important than currency, more important than gold, and that is the confidence of the people. Confidence and courage are the essentials of success in carrying out our plan. You people must have faith; you must not be stampeded by rumors or guesses. Let us unite in banishing fear. We have provided the machinery to restore our financial system; it is up to you to support and make it work. It is your problem no less than it is mine. Together we cannot fail.

[*] Robert S. McElvaine, *The Depression and New Deal: A History in Documents* (New York: Oxford University Press, 2003).

ADDRESSING THE BANK ISSUE

Roosevelt's first move was to impose a national "bank holiday," from March 6 to 13, at which time all banks closed so government inspectors could review their books. Trading on the NYSE and Chicago Board of Trade also was suspended. This was the first time such a move had been made in the United States. Bank failures had become a common occurrence. They generally went out of business when too many loans were not repaid; when they were mismanaged (either on purpose by unscrupulous managers or unintentionally); and when many depositors swarmed to the bank in a panic to withdraw all their funds, an event called a "run."

As Roosevelt explained in an educational fireside chat when announcing that the bank holiday would come to an end on March 13, banks do not keep all of the depositors' cash in their vaults. At any given time, some of it is invested in mortgage loans and other businesses. He promised that certain banks would open the next day and that every day thereafter he would authorize the opening of more banks. He acknowledged that individuals might lose some money, but promised that he would do his best to avoid any unnecessary losses. He told the people that if he did not take this step, there would be more and greater loss of personal wealth. Roosevelt spoke in a calm, rational, and fatherly tone, reassuring his listeners that he had the situation under control. Apparently his message had the desired effect, and when the Philadelphia National Bank reopened—one of the first to do so—its president reported that customers had been receptive and were again making deposits.

Financial assistance was given to those banks that needed it, and those with solid finances were reopened. As the banks again opened their doors, some allowed depositors to withdraw a certain percentage of the money in their accounts. Some banks required the depositor to submit a letter that stated why he or she wanted to withdraw the funds. Roosevelt's decisive action and no-nonsense, truthful approach had restored public confidence.

A NEW DIRECTION

Roosevelt's other programs were sold together as a package—as a "new deal" providing a system to lessen the impact of any future depressions. The first bill passed was the Agricultural Adjustment Act (AAA), which called for the reduction of farm production on certain crops in order to increase demand, thus realizing a higher profit for farmers. The Civilian Conservation Corps (CCC) was established to put unmarried young men between the ages of 18 and 25 to work, mainly planting trees and building dams and other projects. The Civil Works Administration (CWA) was set up to pay workers for manual, unskilled labor. The Public Works Administration (PWA) worked with private businesses to build public works projects, including schools, hospitals, roads, bridges, and sewage systems. The Tennessee Valley Authority (TVA) built 15 large dams in the Tennessee River Valley, providing cheap electricity for millions and controlling floods in that area.

Roosevelt felt that his variety of programs would empower discouraged Americans by putting them back to work. He believed that, by and large, people did not want to be simply taken care of; they did not want to take handouts. He believed, instead, that unemployed Americans wanted one thing—jobs. In other words, he also realized that he needed to stir the cultural melting pot that was America. He needed to unify everyone, and gather their support, for his ideas to work. He and his wife, Eleanor, a smart, strong, and independent woman, reached out to different ethnic groups in various ways, always denouncing any form of racism along the way. During a speech he gave to the conservative organization Daughters of the American Revolution, he said, "Remember, remember always, that all of us, and you and I especially, are descended from immigrants and revolutionists."[11]

Once in office, he also helped break down ethnic barriers by appointing Thomas Walsh of Montana as attorney general and James Farley as postmaster general. The two men were of Irish descent, and at the time the Irish were considered second-class citizens. He appointed Henry Morgenthau Jr., a Jewish man, as

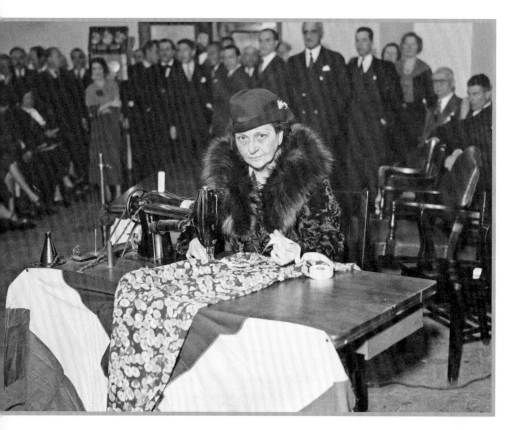

In 1933, Frances Perkins became the first female presidential cabinet member when she was named U.S. secretary of labor by President Franklin Roosevelt. Perkins was responsible for the implementation of many programs and legislation, including the Civilian Conservation Corps and the Social Security Act.

secretary of the treasury, a position Morgenthau held through all four of Roosevelt's terms. Matthew T. Abruzzo of New York City was the first appointed federal judge of Italian descent, and Miecislaus Szuymcak was the first Polish man appointed to the board of governors of the Federal Reserve Bank. Perhaps it was his wife's influence, but Roosevelt also appointed the first woman to the presidential cabinet, Frances Perkins. She was a social worker who advocated a five-day workweek (six days was standard at the time), minimum wage for everyone (it did not exist at the time), and abolition of child labor (even preteens put in long days in factories and mills). And although they were not an official part of the government, Roosevelt gathered a group of black men and one woman to advise him on racial issues. This "black cabinet" included Mary McLeod Bethune, a teacher who acted as an adviser to both the president and Mrs. Roosevelt.

Of course, not everyone agreed that Roosevelt's approach was the right one. He was accused of creating a huge bureaucracy that increased the national debt and failed to balance the federal budget. Detractors called it an "ineffective, expensive experiment." Words and phrases such as, "self-determination," "individual responsibility," and "self-reliance" were used by the New Deal's opponents. They claimed that these American attributes were being destroyed by the ever-increasing reach of the federal government. They believed that government's role should remain very limited and that businesses should be left to rise and fall with the marketplace. They believed that the Great Depression would end on its own, and that a "natural selection" would take place, whereby those businesses and individuals unable to survive would be culled out, leaving the strong and moral to carry on. They stressed increased self-responsibility and encouraged neighbors to help each other.

Yet, as the New Dealers pointed out, there simply was no other way to pull the country out of this depression. Private relief organizations had proven no match for the scope of the disaster, and only the federal government had the resources to save the country. Roosevelt's supporters said the New Deal helped to nearly double national income in seven years, employed millions, and restored the country's morale. These Democrats also attacked the Republican ideals of "rugged individualism" as a "smoke screen" to hide the true Republican agenda of allowing the rich to become richer while forcing the poor to fend for themselves. It will never be known for certain how much worse the Great Depression may have been for the country as a whole if the New Deal had never been implemented. What is known is that these programs put millions to work and restored a measure of self-esteem to the struggling country.

Roosevelt proved to be one of the most popular presidents ever, serving an unprecedented four terms. He was tireless in pursuit of his goals and unwavering in his ideals. His spirit and unflagging energy, in turn, energized a demoralized nation, an intangible asset of the New Deal. His programs not only impacted those living through the Great Depression; many of them continued on and would impact future generations

KEYNESIAN ECONOMICS

Keynesianism is the theory of economics in which both the government and private sector are involved. It advocates using government spending and taxation to affect economic behavior, impacting the overall health of the economy. Franklin D. Roosevelt based many of his proposals on Keynesian economics, and the theory rose in popularity as laissez-faire beliefs were, in turn, rejected.

British economist John Maynard Keynes (1883–1946) is the man for whom the theory is named. Perhaps the leading economist in the world at the time, Keynes advocated government intervention, especially to counteract the negative effects of recessions and depressions. He published the work for which he is most widely known, *General Theory of Employment, Interest, and Money*, in 1936. The book challenged most economic theories of the day, but his ideas became widely accepted as time passed.

Keynes wrote in the *New York Evening Post* on October 25, 1929, "The extraordinary speculation on Wall Street in past months has driven up the rate of interest to an unprecedented level." This statement reflects Keynes's belief that overspeculation and inflated stock prices of Americans. Minimum wage, standard working hours, and improved child labor laws made working conditions safer and better. The country has Roosevelt and the New Deal to thank for improved housing, bank deposit insurance, stock market regulation, aid to families with young children, the federal school lunch program, and Social Security—all social safety nets that citizens did not have before. Undoubtedly mistakes were made, but in any experiment—and the New Deal was indeed called the "great experiment"—mistakes are made on the road to success.

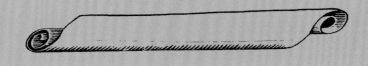

in the months preceding the crash of October 29, 1929, were the prime reasons behind it. (Interestingly, Keynes also lost heavily in the crash.)

John Kenneth Galbraith (1908–2006), a Canadian-American economist, also forecasted the crash. Galbraith agreed with Keynes's theories, was a liberal and progressive, and wrote prolifically about economics for much of his life. He was a professor at Harvard University and served under several presidents, including Franklin D. Roosevelt, Harry S. Truman, John F. Kennedy, and Lyndon B. Johnson. He also received the Presidential Medal of Freedom twice. Galbraith believed that the crash could have been predicted, saying the loss of nearly 90 percent of the market's value between 1929 and 1932 indicated that it was overvalued in 1929. He wrote in 1961, "Early in 1928, the nature of the boom changed. The mass escape into make-believe, so much a part of the true speculative orgy, started in earnest. . . . On the first of January of 1929, as a matter of probability, it was most likely that the boom would end before the year was out."[*]

---

[*] Available online at *www.eh.net/encyclopedia/article/bierman.crash*

Putting the
Program to Work

The social and work programs Franklin Roosevelt established in the early days of his presidency were diverse and all-encompassing, and required Americans to reevaluate the role of government in their lives. President Hoover had believed in giving money to businesses to continue production, but Roosevelt realized that if the people had no money to buy goods, it did not make any sense for businesses to produce. So Roosevelt's goal was twofold: to put people back to work, so, in turn, they could go out and once again begin spending money.

The ideas behind these programs were not complex, but they were daring and bold in the sense that they required people to turn their perceptions of government upside down. It was not easy for proud, independent people to put out their hands and ask for help. Many Americans would rather live on the streets than ask for handouts. Roosevelt recognized and admired these qualities of pride and self-reliance, which is why his proposals did not involve handouts.

NEW DEAL PROGRAMS

Within weeks of President Roosevelt's inauguration on March 4, 1933, Congress passed the Civilian Conservation Corps Reforestation Relief Act, forming the Civilian Conservation Corps (CCC), one of the most popular programs in the New Deal. The CCC, run by the U.S. Army, took applications from unmarried young men between the ages of 18 and 25 whose families were on relief. An initial grant of $300,000 was used to hire the men, who were sent into remote areas of the country to plant new trees in forests that had been logged, constructing new parks and repairing old ones, building reservoirs, and partaking in other projects in rural and wilderness areas.

Those who were accepted were paid $30 per month, of which $25 was sent home to their families. The men were provided shelter, living in barracks or dormitories, and meals, eating in a common mess hall. An added bonus of working with the CCC was social interaction and camaraderie among peers. Artists working for the Works Progress Administration (WPA) created posters showing a smiling young man wielding an ax and speaking of the CCC as "a young man's opportunity for work, play, study, and health." By the end of that summer, 300,000 men were employed in more than 1,000 camps around the country. By the time the program ended in July 1942, 3 million young men had participated in the CCC. Although the program had its detractors, who claimed the camps were too militaristic, its popularity and success were undeniable.

The Federal Emergency Relief Act (FERA) also was passed, creating the Federal Emergency Relief Administration, which handed out $500 million in grants to the states to provide relief to the unemployed through networks of private agencies. The money would pay for work done, as well as provide clothing and food in some cases. The Reconstruction Finance

One of President Franklin D. Roosevelt's earliest New Deal programs was the Civilian Conservation Corps, which was implemented in 1933 and employed 3 million men during its existence. The CCC provided work for young men through conservation programs such as planting trees, fighting forest fires, and maintaining forest roads and trails. Here, 1,800 recruits line up for lunch at a CCC camp at Fort Slocum, New York.

Corporation (RFC), which President Hoover had established in January 1932, provided the funds. Harry Hopkins, a former social worker who believed in work relief rather than direct cash handouts, was appointed administrator of FERA. His organization instituted the Civil Works Administration (CWA) in late 1933 as a temporary measure to get people working during the winter. FERA's responsibilities were taken over by the WPA and the Social Security Administration in 1935.

The CWA never quite realized its potential. It was a huge proposition, costing the government nearly $1 billion during the winter of 1934. Only those men who had registered as unemployed were supposed to be eligible to work under this program, but it was such a huge bureaucracy and so poorly managed, that it became corrupt. The projects usually involved work that was marginally important to begin with, including repairing playgrounds or digging ditches. Often the men who were hired to work on these projects would arrive at the work site to find no tools, or tools that were inappropriate for the job at hand. This program was not as focused and well structured as Roosevelt's other programs, and it was plagued by scandals and accusations of waste. Roosevelt quickly realized that the CWA was not working, and he also realized that he might have inadvertently set the stage for the creation of a perpetual class of people who were willing to do next to nothing and collect relief payments. If this program had been better managed, it may have lasted longer, but Roosevelt discontinued it after about six months.

The Agricultural Adjustment Act was also passed during Roosevelt's first three months in office. It created the Agricultural Adjustment Administration (AAA) within the Department of Agriculture, which gave the government broad reach in reducing crop surplus. Farmers were given financial support, called a subsidy, to ensure that some of their fields were not used. This lowered the supply of certain crops, such as grains and cotton, and thus raised their prices. In addition, nearly 6 million hogs were killed for the similar aim of tilting the balance of supply and demand. It was seen as distasteful and controversial that food was going to waste while thousands starved around the country, and yet Roosevelt felt that it was necessary as a short-term emergency measure.

The Emergency Farm Mortgage Act was passed at the same time. It provided money for the refinancing of farm mortgages through federal land banks and gave farmers additional time to pay their loans at reduced interest rates. Farmers were also given the opportunity to repurchase their former property, which their bank had seized. Congress authorized the sale of $2 million in tax-exempt government bonds to provide the needed funds. The Farm Credit Act helped fledgling farming cooperatives and set up credit unions for farmers through the establishment of a central bank.

During this time, the Tennessee Valley Authority (TVA) was also established; it developed the Tennessee River region, providing flood control, soil conservation, and reforestation. It also brought electricity to the impoverished residents of the Appalachian Mountains and became one of the lasting New Deal programs. In 1933, the Appalachian region was one of the poorest areas in the country. It covered most of Tennessee, parts of Alabama and Mississippi, Georgia, Kentucky, North Carolina, and Virginia. The public eagerly greeted the TVA. During the 1920s, most water and power companies were privately owned, and corruption and high prices were common. People felt that if such utilities were controlled by the government, there would be regulation needed to provide power at reasonable rates. Today, the TVA provides power to about 8.5 million customers.

The Securities Act was also passed in May 1933. It stated that any firms selling stocks and bonds had to file annual financial statements with the Federal Trade Commission (FTC). If they did not, they were open to criminal charges. The act required full disclosure of information about stocks being traded. The Securities Act of 1934 regulated the secondary trading of securities and established the Securities and Exchange Commission (SEC), which regulated the stock market. Joseph Kennedy (President John F. Kennedy's father) was the first chairman of the SEC. He was tasked with identifying and preventing practices that had led to the market's collapse, including speculation by bankers in their own bank's stocks. The SEC put an end to many of the competitive practices that had led to rampant speculation in the stock market. Today, it protects the interests of individual investors by maintaining order in the market and has established regulations to sustain economic stability and growth.

The Public Works Administration (PWA) had a $3.3 billion budget when President Roosevelt signed the National Industrial Recovery Act. Through the PWA, Roosevelt intended to put people back to work so they would once again have money to spend, thus stimulating the economy. He wanted to get as many unemployed men and women back to work as possible before the winter of 1934. He allocated the money to private businesses to work with the states in building public works projects, including schools, hospitals, apartment complexes, roads, bridges, and sewage systems. He also gave millions to the U.S. Navy to build ships. These projects put engineers, office workers, architects, and construction workers back to work. As manufacturing increased, factory workers also went back to the assembly line.

CONTINUING THE NEW DEAL

In his 1935 State of the Union Address, President Roosevelt outlined his three major goals: job security, security for the old and sick, and improved housing. Soon thereafter, he launched another set of reforms that became known as the Second New Deal. These included the Social Security Act, the Works Progress Administration (WPA), the National Industrial Recovery Act, and the National Labor Relations Act, also known as the Wagner Act, named for its author, New York senator Robert F. Wagner.

The Social Security Act was an innovative piece of legislation. For the first time, Americans had some measure of financial security during their old age. An insurance program, Social Security is funded through taxes on a person's salary—taxes paid equally by the employer and employee. Passed in 1935,

(continues on page 74)

THE SOCIAL SECURITY ACT

In a 1935 radio address, U.S. Secretary of Labor Frances Perkins explained the Social Security Act to the American people:

> People who work for a living in the United States of America can join with all other good citizens on this 48th anniversary of Labor Day in satisfaction that the Congress has passed the Social Security Act. This act established unemployment insurance as a substitute for haphazard methods of assistance in periods when men and women willing and able to work are without jobs. It provides for old-age pensions, which mark great progress over the measures upon which we have hitherto depended in caring for those who have been unable to provide for the years when they can no longer work. It also provides security for dependent and crippled children, mothers, the indigent disabled, and the blind.
>
> Old-age benefits in the form of monthly payments are to be paid to individuals who have worked and contributed to the insurance fund in direct proportion to the total wages earned by such individuals in the course of their employment subsequent to 1936. The minimum monthly payment is to be $10, the maximum $85. These payments will begin in the year 1942 and will be to those who have worked and contributed.
>
> Because of difficulty of administration not all employments are covered in this plan at this time so that the law is not entirely complete in coverage, but it is sufficiently broad to cover all normally employed industrial workers.
>
> This vast system of old-age benefits requires contributions both by employer and employee, each to contribute 3 percent of the total wage paid to the employee. This tax, collected by the Bureau of Internal Revenue, will be graduated, ranging from 1 percent in 1937 to the maximum 3 percent in 1939 and thereafter.

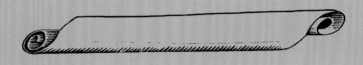

That is, on this man's average income of $100 a month, he will pay to the usual fund three dollars a month and his employer will also pay the same amount over his working years.

In conjunction with the system of old-age benefits, the Act recognizes that unemployment insurance is an integral part of any plan for the economic security of millions of gainfully employed workers. It provides for a plan of cooperative Federal-State action by which a State may enact an insurance system, compatible with Federal requirements and best suited to its individual needs.

It has been necessary, at the present time, to eliminate essentially the same groups from participation under the unemployment insurance plan as in the old-age benefit plan, though it is possible that at some future time a more complete coverage will be formulated.

While it is not anticipated as a complete remedy for the abnormal conditions confronting us at the present time, it is designed to afford protection for the individual against future major economic vicissitudes. It is a sound and reasonable plan and framed with due regard for the present state of economic recovery. It does not represent a complete solution of the problems of economic security, but it does represent a substantial, necessary beginning. It has been developed after careful and intelligent consideration of all the facts and all of the programs that have been suggested or applied anywhere.

This is truly legislation in the interest of the national welfare. We must recognize that if we are to maintain a healthy economy and thriving production, we need to maintain the standard of living of the lower income groups of our population who

(Continues)

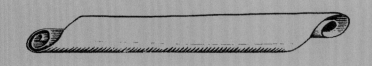

(Continued)

constitute 90 percent of our purchasing power. The President's Committee on Economic Security, of which I had the honor to be chairman, in drawing up the plan, was convinced that its enactment into law would not only carry us a long way toward the goal of economic security for the individual, but also a long way toward the promotion and stabilization of mass purchasing power without which the present economic system cannon endure.

Our social security program will be a vital force working against the recurrence of severe depressions in the future. We can, as the principle of sustained purchasing power in hard times, makes itself felt in every shop, store and mill, grow old without being haunted by the specter of poverty ridden old age or of being a burden on our children.

The passage of this act with so few dissenting votes and with so much intelligent public support is deeply significant of the progress which the American people have made in thought in the social field and awareness of methods of using cooperation through government to overcome social hazards against which the individual alone is inadequate.*

---

* Robert S. McElvaine, *The Depression and New Deal: A History in Documents* (New York: Oxford University Press, 2003), 55–56.

(continued from page 71)

the act originally was intended to also serve as unemployment insurance. Called the Old Age, Survivors and Disability Insurance program, it covered income for retirement, widows, orphans, and the disabled. Unfortunately, it excluded domestic

The Works Progress Administration was another New Deal program instituted in 1935 by President Roosevelt. More than 8.5 million people worked for the WPA during its eight-year existence in such endeavors as building roads and bridges. Another project was the attempted eradication of the white-fringed beetle, which does significant damage to crops in the south.

workers (such as housekeepers) and farmworkers, including migrants, from collecting benefits. This exclusion eliminated many working women and nonwhites.

The WPA was Roosevelt's attempt to get money back into the pockets of the people without putting them on welfare. He firmly believed that handing money to people without requiring work in return damaged their initiative and self-respect. The WPA, sometimes called a "work relief" program, involved a diversity of projects for all kinds of workers. From seamstresses to road engineers to artists and writers to educators, the WPA had them all. Thousands learned to read and write, and immigrants were encouraged to research their histories through WPA teachers. This program did a lot to advance the economic status of women during the 1930s. Mostly widows, single women, and women whose husbands could not find work found jobs with the WPA, which helped increase not only their income, but also their sense of self-esteem and confidence in their ability to care for themselves. More than 3 million Americans worked within the WPA at its height, and a total of 8.5 million people worked in the program over its life span. The majority of the public agreed with Roosevelt that it was better to put people to work, even if they worked at tasks that were solely created for them, than to hand out cash. In fact, 74 percent favored jobs rather than direct relief payments. Lasting for eight years, the WPA provided a psychological lift, not to mention a steady income, for men and women who had been jobless for years.

The National Recovery Administration (NRA) was formed around a sweeping set of legislation—the National Industrial Recovery Act—that required cooperation among business and industry, the government, and the public. At the time, it seemed to be the most innovative program of all of Roosevelt's initiatives because of that cooperative spirit. In some respects it was also a program that involved both political parties, because it drew on some of Herbert Hoover's concepts.

At the NRA's core was a need for economic balance that required planning and the already-mentioned cooperation. One of the first initiatives created under the NRA was to have businesses within each industry write a joint code setting rules regulating wages, hours, child labor, quality of materials, and more. Some felt it was too restrictive. Some argued it was unconstitutional. The automobile and coal mining industries were two groups that resisted compliance with the laws, although both finally gave in during the summer of 1933. Henry Ford was the only business owner in these two industries to remain outside the code, because he chose not to cooperate with the program.

Led by General Hugh Johnson, the NRA used patriotism and symbolism to encourage businessmen to join. A blue eagle served as its logo, and signs stating "We Do Our Part" were posted prominently by businesses that cooperated with the NRA. Parades and songs were two other ways Johnson sold his program to the public. These strategies were initially successful, as production and employment rose throughout the summer. Unfortunately, the higher prices of goods—due to lack of competition—discouraged consumers, and conditions returned to their former state by late fall.

By the spring of 1934, the NRA was under attack from several quarters. Politicians felt the program was like a dictatorship; industry resented the government's interference in their business; unions had not fared as well as they had expected, because private businesses had formed company unions as a way of subverting the unions' efforts for recruitment; and finally, consumers balked at higher prices.

The act was overturned and the administration closed when the U.S. Supreme Court found that it infringed on states' authority and gave legislative powers to the executive branch of the government. The National Labor Relations Act was signed into law in early July 1935. It gave workers the right to organize, forming unions that would bargain with employers for better wages, hours, and working conditions. It also prohibited employers from interfering with the unionization of workers and established the National Labor Relations Board as an independent agency to oversee union elections and prevent unfair labor practices. As mentioned previously, it was also known as the Wagner Act, named for its primary supporter, Senator Robert Wagner of New York. The act gave unions plenty of room to organize and lobby for better working conditions for their members, without fear of retaliation by angry employers.

Roosevelt's programs touched on every sector of American life, from social support networks, to business and industry. He was widely supported and respected by the common man; although he met with some opposition from businessmen and politicians. In spite of some who would have gladly replaced him, he continued to lead the country into the second half of the 1930s, broadening his programs, staying true to his ideals, and leading his country out of the Great Depression.

America at Odds

President Roosevelt's New Deal programs and the continuing initiatives of the Second New Deal gained him friends and foes alike. Given the fact that he was reelected three times, Roosevelt obviously had plenty of backers who believed, as he did, that the New Deal would actually save capitalism rather than destroy it. But he had detractors as well, including many wealthy businessmen who felt the unemployed were simply lazy, and they were quite vocal in their dislike of Roosevelt and his ideas.

But there were industrialists who agreed with him, too, including those in the emerging fields of filmmaking and business machinery. They understood that the New Deal programs were a work in progress, that success was not expected to happen overnight. They also believed that the programs were not meant to address problems of the past, but to address those faced in the present, and those to come in the future. As the country moved from an agricultural-based society to one whose economy was based on industrialization and mechanization, different problems arose and a new approach had to be adopted. In addition to these liberal-minded leaders of industry, Roosevelt could count on the majority of workingmen, middle class, and poor to stand behind him.

OPPOSITION TO ROOSEVELT'S PROGRAMS

Still, some opposition to government economic intervention was growing within a group of industrialists, bankers, and corporations. In 1934, a group called the American Liberty League was formed by conservative Democrats to challenge Roosevelt's ideas. These men included Al Smith, one of Roosevelt's rivals for the Democratic presidential nomination in 1932; Representative Jouett Shouse of Kansas; and John Jakob Raskob, former Democratic National Committee chairman. They joined many industrialists in arguing that the Roosevelt administration was leading the country down a road toward socialism, bankruptcy, and dictatorship. They claimed that people were losing their sense of individual accountability. The league raised and spent millions of dollars promoting their ideas. Funding came from wealthy, successful corporations, such as DuPont, U.S. Steel, General Motors, Standard Oil, and Goodyear Tire and Rubber Company. They and their supporters campaigned for the Republican Party in the presidential election of 1936.

The league's mission stated that it was a nonpartisan organization aiming to

> defend and uphold the Constitution and to disseminate
> information that would teach the necessity of respect for
> the rights of persons and property as fundamental to every
> successful form of government, and will teach the duty of
> government to encourage and protect individual and group
> initiative and enterprise, to foster the right to work, earn,

Big corporations, such as U.S. Steel and General Motors, opposed the Wagner Act, which eliminated employer interference in labor unions. Here, miners and steelworkers march down a street in Farrell, Pennsylvania, on May 1, 1937, to celebrate the upholding of the Wagner Act by the U.S. Supreme Court.

save and acquire property, and to preserve the ownership and lawful use of property when acquired.[12]

The league claimed that Social Security would "mark the end of democracy," and that the Agricultural Adjustment Administration would lead to government control of agriculture. They even brought a court challenge claiming the Wagner

Act was unconstitutional. The Supreme Court upheld the validity of the act in 1937, and the league disbanded in 1940.

As the Great Depression continued, European-born political concepts, including Communism and Fascism, began to gain a foothold among the American people. Desperate people will believe in ideas and do things they might never consider otherwise. The Great Experiment was working for many, but not for all, and the promise of renewed economic and social stability looked promising to some. Although few Americans wanted to embrace the tenets of either Communism or Fascism, their promises of order and discipline did appeal to some common men desperate to find solutions to the poverty and hopelessness that surrounded them. In Europe, these movements were more successful, perhaps in part because, in the years leading up to World War II, the poverty and hopelessness there were even greater than in the United States.

Roosevelt was also attacked by others for not doing enough. Three of his most notable detractors were a Catholic priest, Charles Coughlin of Michigan, Senator Huey Long of Louisiana, and Francis Townsend, a retired medical doctor from California. Each man proposed simple plans to solve the complex problems facing the country, and it was their very simplicity that appealed to the masses.

Father Coughlin, known as the Radio Priest, used his program to call for radical changes that included having the government take over control of all banks. He appealed to a large and diverse audience by supporting Roosevelt's programs, while at the same time preaching that they did not go far enough. His proposals only partially veiled his anti-Semitism and pro-Fascist leanings. In 1942, the Catholic Church ordered him to end his radio program, and he returned to being a parish priest.

Senator Long wanted the government to give every family $2,500 per year, nearly $1,000 more than the average annual salary at the time. His slogan "Every man, a king" inspired many poor people to support him. Long was governor of his state from 1928 to 1932 and a U.S. senator from 1932 to 1935. He was known as a "benevolent dictator"—a dictator for the near absolute control he wielded while in office and benevolent for his attention to the poor among his constituents. He was widely admired for his advocacy of redistributing the state's wealth among the poor. He founded the Share the Wealth Society in 1934, and his popularity grew to such heights that he represented a credible threat to Roosevelt's bid for reelection in 1936. But before that could happen, he was assassinated in 1935 by one of his own constituents who disagreed with his views.

Dr. Francis Townsend believed that the government should pay $200 per month to anyone over age 60. He set up a national organization called Old Age Revolving Pensions, Ltd., to support his plan and collected 20 million signatures on petitions endorsing it. This movement began with a simple letter to the editor of the *Long Beach Press-Telegram* in September 1933, in which he advocated forced retirement at age 60, with the new retirees receiving the $200 bonus, which they were required to spend to invigorate the economy and limit the size of the workforce. In the days before Social Security, a person was either lucky enough to work for one of the few companies offering pensions, had saved enough money while working to pay for expenses during retirement, or had worked until he could not work any longer and often counted on family for care in old age. Farmers and laborers, for example, rarely had enough money to retire. They worked as long as they could and then had to depend on their children or other relatives to care for them.

LABOR UNIONS

Labor unions experienced big changes throughout the 1930s. At the beginning of the Great Depression, unions were no longer popular. They had been losing members throughout the 1920s because, although the country was prosperous as a whole, unemployment remained high. The unemployed could not risk drawing attention to themselves by organizing and striking, because they had no boss against whom to protest. And when there were 100 men ready to work for every available position, the employed could not risk losing their jobs. In addition, wages were so low that it was difficult to pay union dues. But as the positive effects of the New Deal programs began to be felt, unions expanded, adding more members throughout the mid-1930s than at any other time. Men had renewed initiative, because they were once again working. With raised spirits and recognition of class divisions, they were more supportive of the unions' attempts to work as a group to ensure improved working conditions.

As the Great Depression wore on, hunger riots and marches became common. A famous protest was held in 1932, when thousands marched to the Ford Motor Company offices outside Detroit, Michigan, to ask Henry Ford to hire back the men he had laid off. The protest turned into a deadly riot when police were called in and four men were killed. This event turned into an opportunity for union organizers, who used the men's funerals as a chance to preach union ideals. Labor unions turned militant in 1934, calling for strikes to increase membership and force employers to comply with sections of the National Labor Relations Act. Well over one million workers went on strike in 1934, with some strikes turning violent. One such episode of violence was a strike in Minneapolis, Minnesota, by the local organization of the Brotherhood of Teamsters. That union led a strike to shut down the transportation system to end the practice of an "open shop." This practice meant that workers were not allowed to form unions, which was in direct opposition to NLRA regulations. Two men were killed during this strike. Similarly, a dockworkers' strike that summer in San Francisco ended in bloodshed.

In addition to the National Labor Relations Act, the American Federation of Labor (AFL), which formerly encompassed unions representing various craft workers, changed its structure to also

During the four-day West Coast Longshore Strike of 1934, San Francisco police killed Howard F. Sperry and Nicholas Bordoise, both of whom were picketing in support of the strike. Here, mourners march down San Francisco's Market Street during the slain men's funeral procession.

represent industrial workers. One of its branches, the Congress of Industrial Organizations (CIO), had recently been created to represent the steel, automobile, and rubber industries. The two organizations merged in 1955, forming the AFL-CIO, which today represents 9 million American workingmen and women within 53 individual unions, in occupations as diverse as teachers, miners, engineers, and doctors.

Even the agriculture industry organized—with mixed results. Farmers had endured a one-third loss in income in the three years following the stock market crash. This loss added insult to the injury they had suffered throughout the entire 1920s. By 1933, a group of Midwest farmers called the Farmers' Holiday Association had organized and found some interesting ways to make themselves heard. They often blocked trucks carrying livestock and produce from getting to market. By declaring a "farmer's holiday," similar to a "bank holiday," this group attempted to drive up prices by withholding goods, so prices would go up as supply decreased and demand increased. Sometimes farmers would hold "penny auctions." When the farm mortgage company came to auction the land of a farmer who could not repay his loan, his neighbors would show up, armed, to intimidate anyone who would bid a legitimate amount for the property. Sometimes they would hang nooses as further proof that a high bid would be met with a higher price. A penny or two would be bid for the farm, which was then turned over to the original farmer.

Farmers initially endorsed the actions of the Agricultural Adjustment Administration, but did not always agree with how they were carried out. In September 1933, Secretary of Agriculture Henry Wallace ordered that 10 million acres of cotton be plowed under and that more than 200,000 pigs be slaughtered because overproduction was driving prices so low that farmers could not survive on what money they were making. Destroying this food source and valuable crop when people were starving was a moral sticking point, even though Wallace formed an organization—the Federal Surplus Relief Corporation—to distribute the meat.

The decade of the Great Depression was a strange and desperate time that called for bold and drastic measures. President Roosevelt was brave enough to take the necessary steps, with the support of the majority of his countrymen.

Popular Culture

All Americans suffered to some degree during the Great Depression. Their suffering and coping mechanisms, as well as traditional American values such as self-determination, self-reliance, and optimism, were reflected in the popular culture of the 1930s. Movies came into their own during the depression, and some believe it was the Golden Age of Hollywood. At the start of the depression, "talkies" were a novelty. By the time the depression was coming to an end, Americans were entranced by lavish musicals and epics in color.

In the earliest days of the Great Depression, theaters had to drastically reduce prices to keep people coming. But movies came to be an inexpensive way to escape reality, and whoever could save on the cost of admission would welcome a couple hours away from reality. By the end of the decade, an average of 80 million tickets were sold every week.

Dorothea Lange's famous 1936 photograph of Florence Thompson and her children, entitled *Migrant Mother,* represents the contrast between grinding poverty and the strength of the human spirit. Thompson, who died in 1983 at the age of 80, was just 32 at the time this photo was taken.

Blockbuster musicals reflected renewed hope and dramatic epics reminded viewers they weren't struggling alone. Nearly all the films produced at this time reflected the country's changing value system. Some of the biggest movies of the 1930s were

Little Caesar (1930); *Dracula* (1931); *Duck Soup* (1933); *Mr. Smith Goes to Washington* (1939); *The Wizard of Oz* (1939); *Gone with the Wind* (1939); and, perhaps the most timely and realistic movie of the era, *The Grapes of Wrath* (1940), based on the classic John Steinbeck novel.

Two board games that are still popular today were invented during the Great Depression. One was Monopoly. It seems contradictory that a game about earning money and bankrupting your competitor would become so popular during an economic depression. Perhaps it was an escape from reality, or maybe the possibility of getting rich, even using fake money, was its allure. Another game invented during the depression was Scrabble. This famous and well-loved word game was invented by an unemployed architect who wanted to create a game requiring good vocabulary skills with the element of chance. The legions of Scrabble fans have grown over the years, and tournaments, special dictionaries, and clubs can be found throughout the country.

ART, MUSIC, LITERATURE, AND SPORTS

The exuberant music and behavior of the 1920s was reflected in the artistic movements of that decade, with abstract and modern paintings in vogue. In just such a way, the gritty truth of day-to-day American life during the Great Depression was reflected in its art, known as "The American Scene." Paintings and sculptures were realistic, with a touch of idealism. Painters, sculptors, and photographers had a wealth of subject matter, and their work remains popular today as a visual record of the era. Two of the most prolific photographers were Dorothea Lange and Walker Evans, whose stark photographs revealed a grinding poverty balanced by the strength of the human spirit.

Reading, as always, remained a convenient way to escape from reality. During the 1930s, several notable new writers emerged on the scene. One, Theodor Seuss Geisel (Dr. Seuss), became one of the most beloved children's authors. His first book, *And to Think I Saw It on Mulberry Street*, was published in 1936. It

In 1939, author John Steinbeck wrote his third novel, the Pulitzer Prize–winning *Grapes of Wrath*. Set during the Great Depression, the novel portrays the dire conditions experienced by a family of sharecroppers as they are forced to leave the dust bowl of Oklahoma and move to California.

was about a young boy who uses his imagination to change a horse and wagon into an extraordinary beast. John Steinbeck is perhaps the best-known adult novelist to write about the Great Depression. His books, although works of fiction, used his keen eye for observation and detail to reflect the experiences of those around him. His 1936 novel, *In Dubious Battle*, was about a fruit pickers' strike in California. *Of Mice and Men* was published the following year and detailed the experiences of two men whose dreams were destroyed by the drought in the Midwest. His third novel, *The Grapes of Wrath* (1939), clearly transmitted how hope for the future and love of family could hold a family together as they migrated westward in search of a better life.

Many other authors who remain popular today published during the depression era. Margaret Mitchell's 1936 novel, *Gone with the Wind*, although set during the Civil War, spoke of the same type of deprivation and survival skills that depression era families were forced to use. Some of Ernest Hemingway's most popular works were also published in the 1930s; they include *Death in the Afternoon*, *Green Hills of Africa*, and *To Have and Have Not*. Pearl S. Buck's Pulitzer Prize–winning novel, *The Good Earth*, was published in 1931. Aldous Huxley, best known for his 1932 novel, *Brave New World*, speculated on the downfall of civilization several centuries in the future.

In the world of comics, two well-loved superheroes were also "born" during the Great Depression, and one little redhaired girl moved into the nation's hearts. Superman was dreamed up by two teens from Cleveland. He debuted in 1938 as a champion of the oppressed. His character has spawned TV shows, movies, and all types of toys, without losing any of his original appeal. Batman came out a year later. Both he and Superman reflect the New Deal liberalism of the day, with Batman reflecting President Roosevelt as a wealthy man who adopts a different persona to fight injustice. Finally, Little Orphan Annie demonstrated that the super rich could still be "good guys," as Daddy Warbucks, her benefactor, rescued her from a life as a poor orphan and helped her fight villains.

The decade's music also reflected both the highs and lows of the Great Depression, as hope again appeared on the horizon. It ran the gamut from soulful blues and spirituals to bouncy tunes meant to keep one humming while one worked. The song "Blue Skies," released in 1927, was all about the shining days of the optimistic 1920s; "Stormy Weather" (1933) was the exact opposite: "Don't know why there's no sun up in the sky . . . Life is bare, gloom and misery everywhere . . . ." And then there was the classic theme song from 1939's *Wizard of Oz*. Sung by Judy Garland, "Over the Rainbow" promised that better days lay ahead if one could only believe.

The most popular sports of the depression era were boxing, baseball, and football. Household names from back then are still recognizable today: Lou Gehrig, Babe Ruth, Joe DiMaggio, and Joe Louis. Two black sports stars of the decade proved that racist attitudes were still very much a part of society. The first was Jesse Owens, who won four gold medals at the 1936 Berlin Olympics. As Hitler and his racist policies were growing, Owens forced the world to recognize his talent. The second was Joe Louis, who fought German boxer Max Schmeling in the late 1930s. Backing the black American over the white German, Americans began a subtle shift in attitude toward African Americans.

Lessons Learned

Even the most highly trained financial minds of the time did not forecast the stock market crash of October 29, 1929. If these economists did not see it coming, how could the common, small investor? And more importantly, how might an economic disaster on this scale be predicted and prevented in the future?

By September 1929, the stock buying frenzy that had characterized the previous several years had reached its peak. Several small events occurred during that month that left a few savvy investors and President Herbert Hoover warning against rampant buying. But very few heeded the warnings. No one wanted the party to end.

As flappers danced away the night during the Jazz Age, bootleggers manufactured bathtub gin, speculators borrowed money to buy stocks, and consumerism rose to new heights. Every housewife had to have the newest vacuum cleaner, refrigerator, toaster, and other modern conveniences that would make her life easier.

The introduction of electricity to most urban areas by the 1920s also allowed for radios to become a common fixture in most living rooms and parlors. The former American practice of frugality and saving for a rainy day gave way to a new mind-set: buy what you want, when you want it, using borrowed money. The idea of buying on credit entered the stock market, as brokers extended credit to investors who were willing to buy on margin, figuring that stock values would continue to rise, and they could then sell their stocks at a profit and pay off their loans. The glittery, fun, prosperous 1920s lulled the populace into a false sense of security.

But under the surface, trouble was brewing on several quarters. During the 1920s, the agricultural industry began to struggle, due in part to the return of European farmers to their fields following World War I. After losing the European market, American farm surpluses grew until their profits barely allowed them to survive—and often did not even provide for that. In addition, the weather was not cooperative during this period. A series of droughts, followed by floods, left farmers with ruined produce, that is if crops would even grow at all. Farming methods at the time ripped away the top layers of soil from the earth, paving the way for the sandstorms that caused the area to become known as the Dust Bowl by the mid-1930s.

The American economy of the 1920s grew weaker as production continued, even as demand for consumer goods slowed. As a result, job layoffs were just around the corner for these industries that would soon see their warehouses full of merchandise they could barely give away.

During this period, there were few regulations concerning banking practices and stock trading. Bankers would often use depositors' money to speculate in the market, hoping to strike it rich. They would then replace the money, and no one would be the wiser. Near the beginning of his first administration, President Franklin Roosevelt quickly established laws governing banking and stocks. His laws are the kind that should help prevent another massive crash of the market.

DUST STORM APPROACHING SPEARMAN, TEXAS APRIL 14, 1935

During the early 1930s, much of the Great Plains became a dust bowl due to years of overcultivation of crops, poor land management, and severe drought. Huge dust storms, like the one pictured here near Spearman, Texas, became the norm, because the soil was no longer anchored by the long grass native to the region.

The stock market has always been unpredictable and will always contain a measure of volatility. The year 1929 was not the first time the market crashed, nor would it be the last. On October 19, 1987, the stock market lost 25 percent of its value in one day, with the industrial average dropping 508 points. This drop ended a five-year bull market in which the industrial average had risen to a high of 2,722 in August of that year. When the market took a dive in 1987, the Federal Reserve

(continues on page 98)

**ONE MAN'S EXPERIENCE
DURING THE GREAT DEPRESSION**

The following was excerpted from a story by Kenneth Bruckart, which appeared in the March/April 2006 issue of *Reminisce* magazine. In the story, Bruckart tells how his father's honesty during the Great Depression was ultimately rewarded:

I was born in Washington, D.C., in 1925. My dad, William L. Bruckart, was a newspaper reporter for the now-defunct *United States Daily,* which subsequently became *U.S. News and World Report* magazine.

In the spring of 1933, Dad was also a syndicated columnist for the Western Newspaper Union, and an accredited member of the White House Correspondents group of reporters. The group was initiated by President Franklin Delano Roosevelt to provide a means of communicating with the public when he had something special to say.

One morning the reporters were called to the Oval Office. The President told them that he had something to say that was strictly confidential, and that each person there was on his personal honor not to use or disclose the information until the banks of the nation had a chance to bring their business to an orderly close.

This was to preempt any more panic than was already fairly widespread regarding the number of banks failing across the country. Roosevelt announced to the newsmen early in the day so they could get their stories in print in time for the evening editions of their papers.

He said that all banks would be closed until emergency actions could be taken to secure them. This was a critical time. Many banks had made too many loans to too many financially risky people, and the banks did not have enough cash on hand to pay depositors their money back on demand.

Time was needed for the federal government to arrange for sound banks to take over defaulted banks and for the government

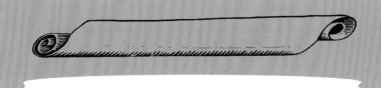

to get more cash dollars into the hands of remaining banks to stop the panicky withdrawals.

All my family's worldly goods rested in the Riggs National Bank, directly across the street from the White House. All Dad would have had to do was cross the street, withdraw our money and go home.

However, Dad went to a pay phone near the White House and called Mother. He told her what had just transpired and asked her what he should do, adding he had given the President his word of honor not to use or disclose the information.

Mother was silent for a minute before she said, "Bill, you must do what you think is best for all concerned, and whatever you decide, I'm with you all the way."

Dad replied, "Well, I guess I'd better get the story in, and then I'll be coming on home."

And that is how we lost all we had.

But that's not the end of the story. Two weeks later, Dad was told by the syndicate that he would have to go without a salary for a while—it turned out to be a whole year—but that if he continued his weekly column, he would eventually be reimbursed.

When Mr. Mudd, our local vegetable man (and friend) came around in his pickup truck the next week, Mother told him we wouldn't be buying any vegetables for a while because we had no money. He drew a roll of bills out of his pocket and handed Mother $500! He told her that he didn't trust banks, and so he had all his money safe and sound.

We did take the money and we did repay it eventually. It kept us alive until Dad could find other work. We did a lot of things to survive during the Depression, as did many others, but we all helped each other, and survive we did.

(continued from page 95)

Board acted immediately, loaning money, and buying stock, so banks and businesses would not go bankrupt.

Another dip in the market came in the fall of 2000, when stocks within the technology sector lost more than $3 million in value. This drop was caused by rampant buying of "dot-com" stocks—the name for companies that did business solely on the Internet. The slowdown led to a worldwide recession in the spring of 2001. On September 11, 2001, the day of the terrorist attacks on New York City and Washington, D.C., the industrial average fell by 684 points and the market was closed for six days.

Still, the United States had never experienced such a prolonged period of economic downturn as the Great Depression, and hasn't since. By the time President Roosevelt took the oath of office on March 4, 1933, 25 percent of the American workforce was unemployed. That was more than 13 million men and women. The former middle class of merchants and professionals felt the pinch the most. The Great Depression hit everyone hard, although some quarters of the population had previously been poor and disenfranchised, namely, blacks, immigrants, Native Americans, Mexicans, and Filipinos.

Those who had bet everything on the continued success of the stock market, believing that stock values would continue to rise at an astronomical pace, found themselves and their families penniless. Furniture and family belongings were sold to repay brokers, pay rent, and put food on the table. Once everything was gone, if the man of the house was still lucky enough to have his job, the family struggled by from paycheck to paycheck. If he was among the Americans who were out of work, he might have made the difficult choice to send one or more of his children to live with relatives while he and his wife searched for work or begged.

Americans had always taken care of their own. Government interference in private lives had never occurred. Private relief agencies existed to supplement the extended family, which often included several generations under one roof, but these agencies could not keep up with the influx of the needy through their doors. The day after Roosevelt took office, he instituted a series of programs, laws, and agencies designed to counteract the poverty, joblessness, and hopelessness running rampant throughout the country. During his so-called First 100 Days, he passed an unprecedented number of laws, some of which are still with us today.

Probably the most popular program was the Civilian Conservation Corps (CCC), which provided work for young men between the ages of 18 and 25 in construction and reforestation projects in rural and wilderness areas of the country. The men lived and worked in military-like conditions, sharing barracks and a mess hall. Of the $30 they were paid each month, $25 was sent home to their families, who were on government relief.

The Federal Emergency Relief Act was passed, which provided $500 million in grants to states to provide relief to the needy through networks of private agencies. FERA started the Civil Works Administration in late 1933 as a temporary measure to get people to work that winter. The CWA lasted only about six months because of mismanagement and inefficient use of funds and manpower. The Works Progress Administration (WPA) was another of Roosevelt's attempts at a work relief program that provided jobs for people. The WPA employed people in all occupations throughout the country and was much more successful than the CWA. WPA workers included artists, photographers, teachers, engineers, and others. It was a program that has provided a legacy of photographs and books from that era; it taught thousands to learn to write; and helped women gain a stronger economic foothold.

The Agricultural Adjustment Act also was passed, establishing the Agricultural Adjustment Administration (AAA) within the Department of Agriculture. Farmers were given subsidies to let fields lay unused or to plow under crops, as well as to slaughter millions of pigs. Although these acts—wasting food when millions were starving—were criticized, they were seen as necessary short-term measures to equalize farm production with demand. (The meat was distributed to the poor through an affiliated agency.) Like some aspects of AAA policies, not all of Roosevelt's programs and theories were met with enthusiasm by everyone. He had his detractors, especially after the economy began to show some signs of recovery by the middle of the decade. Perhaps his political opponents felt threatened when the programs they attacked turned out to be working. But he appealed to the common man, especially through his weekly series of radio addresses, known as "fireside chats." He had a talent for appearing to know each person like a true friend, and spoke through the radio as a trusted confidant. His wife, Eleanor, helped in his efforts by moving around the country, making speeches, investigating the success of various New Deal initiatives, and encouraging a more equal approach to treatment for minorities and women.

LASTING NEW DEAL PROGRAMS

Many of Roosevelt's New Deal programs were designed to provide quick relief to individuals and businesses and to get people back to work. But, as has been stated, some of his measures were meant to permanently reform how business was done and to create long-term safety nets to help the less fortunate.

The Securities Act of 1933 established rules to regulate the buying and selling of stocks. Brokerage houses had to file annual financial statements and provide full disclosure about any stocks being traded. The Securities Act of 1934 regulated the secondary trading of securities and established the Securities and Exchange Commission (SEC), which to this day regulates the stock market. The SEC ended many of the competitive practices that had contributed to the rampant speculation of the 1920s.

The Tennessee Valley Authority (TVA) is another New Deal program still in existence. It developed the Tennessee River region, providing flood control, soil conservation, and reforestation to a wide swath of land covering seven states. It also provided inexpensive electricity to this area.

Under the New Deal, the U.S. government established the Tennessee Valley Authority in 1933. The program was created to control floods along the Tennessee River and also bring electricity to the region. Here, deliverymen bring an electric stove and washing machine to a rural farm in Tennessee in the 1940s.

Finally, the Social Security Act was originally intended as an old-age and unemployment insurance program. It covered income for retirees, widows, orphans, and the disabled. It was funded through taxes on a person's paycheck, shared by the employer and the employee.

The Great Depression finally ended when the United States entered World War II in 1941. Production geared up to build arms and other wartime provisions, people went back to work, and the economy began to thrive again. The carefree days of the 1920s were gone forever, but in their place was a more mature country with social safety nets and banking and stock trading safety nets that would protect the country over the coming years.

CHRONOLOGY

1928 **October** During presidential campaign, Herbert Hoover gives his "rugged individualism" speech in New York City.

1928 **November** Hoover is elected president, defeating Alfred E. Smith by a wide margin.

1929 **October** The stock market crashes, followed by a severe depression.

1930 **December** Many banks have failed, including the Bank of the United States (62 branches and 400,000

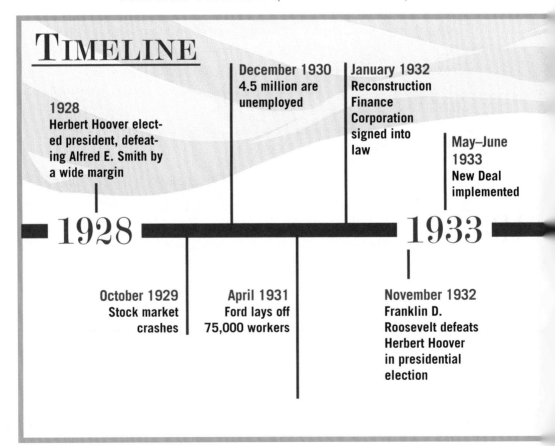

TIMELINE

1928
Herbert Hoover elected president, defeating Alfred E. Smith by a wide margin

December 1930
4.5 million are unemployed

January 1932
Reconstruction Finance Corporation signed into law

May–June 1933
New Deal implemented

1928 ——— **1933**

October 1929
Stock market crashes

April 1931
Ford lays off 75,000 workers

November 1932
Franklin D. Roosevelt defeats Herbert Hoover in presidential election

depositors in New York City); 4.5 million are unemployed; severe drought hits Midwest and South; Hoover asks Congress for $150 million to help the unemployed.

1931   **April** Carmaker Henry Ford lays off 75,000 workers from his factories; "Brother Can You Spare a Dime?" is a popular song as unemployment rises; drought worsens; bank closings continue; social service agencies run out of money.

1932   **January** Reconstruction Finance Corporation signed into law to lend money to banks, businesses, cities, and states to stimulate business activity.

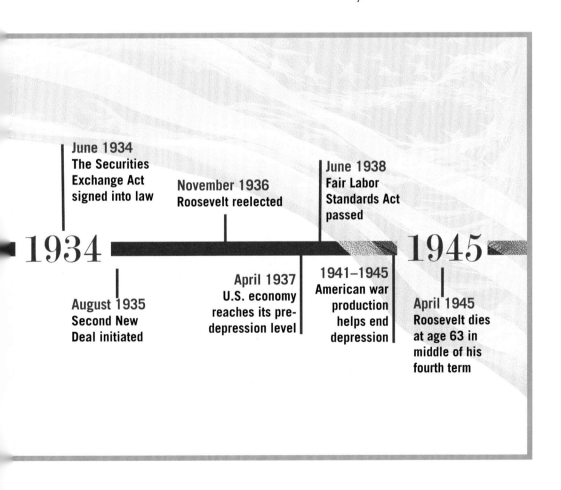

June 1934
The Securities
Exchange Act
signed into law

November 1936
Roosevelt reelected

June 1938
Fair Labor
Standards Act
passed

1934

August 1935
Second New
Deal initiated

April 1937
U.S. economy
reaches its pre-
depression level

1941–1945
American war
production
helps end
depression

1945

April 1945
Roosevelt dies
at age 63 in
middle of his
fourth term

1932   **Spring** Thousands of WWI veterans march to
        Washington, D.C., demanding promised monetary
        bonuses for their war service.

1932   **July** Franklin Delano Roosevelt receives Democratic
        nomination for president.

1932   **September** Roosevelt gives a speech in which he says
        that all citizens are owed a right to life and a measure
        of security and happiness by the federal government.

1932   **November** Roosevelt defeats Hoover in a landslide,
        winning the electoral vote by 472 to 59.

1933   **March** Unemployment is at 15 million when Roosevelt
        is inaugurated as thirty-second president on March 4;
        closes banks for one week, and orders an examination
        of their record books; gives his first fireside chat;
        Agricultural Adjustment Act (AAA) and Civilian
        Conservation Corps (CCC) are proposed, marking
        the beginning of the New Deal.

1933   **May–June** New Deal implemented; business gradually
        picks up as government programs give jobs to many
        who had been unemployed.

1933   **December** The Twenty-First Amendment is ratified,
        repealing Prohibition.

1934   **June** The Securities Exchange Act is signed into law,
        initiating federal regulation of trading practices.

1934   **July** Federal Communications Commission is created,
        regulating radio, telegraph and cable businesses;
        National Housing Act is passed.

1935   **August** The second New Deal is initiated, including the
        Social Security Act and the Wagner Act.

1935	**September** Louisiana senator Huey Long is assassinated in Baton Rouge.
1936	**February** Agricultural Adjustment Act is declared unconstitutional by the Supreme Court.
1936	**November** Roosevelt is reelected, defeating Alf Landon by an electoral margin of 523 to 8.
1937	**April** The strength of the U.S. economy reaches its pre-depression level.
1937	**May** The Social Security Act and the Wagner Act are upheld by the Supreme Court.
1938	**June** New public works projects implemented to fight recession; Fair Labor Standards Act is passed; second Agricultural Adjustment Act is passed.
1939	**September** Former Roosevelt adviser Raymond Moley publishes *After Seven Years,* criticizing president and New Deal; Germany invades Poland.
1941–1945	United States enters WWII; American war production helps to end Great Depression.
1945	**April** President Franklin Roosevelt dies at age 63 in middle of his fourth term; succeeded by Harry Truman.

NOTES

CHAPTER 2

1. Adrian A. Paradis, *The Hungry Years: The Story of the Great American Depression* (Philadelphia: Chilton Book Co., 1967), 11.

CHAPTER 3

2. Don Nardo, *The Great Depression* (San Diego, Calif.: Green Haven Press, 1997), 8.
3. Alex Woolf, *The Wall Street Crash* (New York: Raintree/Steck-Vaughn Publishers, 2003), 20.
4. Ibid., 24.

CHAPTER 4

5. Paradis, 26–27.
6. Ibid., 30.
7. Nardo, 15.

CHAPTER 5

8. Robert S. McElvaine, *The Depression and New Deal: A History in Documents* (New York: Oxford University Press, 2003), 45.
9. William Loren Katz, *A History of Multicultural America: The New Freedom to the New Deal* (Austin, Tex.: Steck-Vaughn, 1993), 60.

CHAPTER 6

10. Nardo, 17.
11. Katz, 65.

CHAPTER 8

12. McElvaine, 60.

BIBLIOGRAPHY

Collier, Christopher, and James Lincoln Collier. *Progressivism, The Great Depression, and The New Deal 1901–1941.* New York: Benchmark Books/Marshall Cavendish, 2001.

Katz, William Loren. *A History of Multicultural America: The New Freedom to the New Deal.* Austin, Tex.: Steck-Vaughn Publishers, 1993.

Nardo, Don. *The Great Depression.* San Diego, Calif.: Green-haven Press, 1997.

Paradis, Adrian A. *The Hungry Years: The Story of the Great American Depression.* Philadelphia: Chilton Book Co., 1967.

Woolf, Alex. *The Wall Street Crash.* New York: Raintree/Steck-Vaughn, 2003.

FURTHER READING

Galbraith, John Kenneth. *The Great Crash, 1929.* Boston: Houghton Mifflin, 1997.

Hiebert, Ray Eldon. *The Stock Market Crash of 1929: Panic on Wall Street Ends the Jazz Age.* New York: F. Watts, 1970.

Klein, Maury. *Rainbow's End: The Crash of 1929.* New York: Oxford University Press, 2001.

Kyvig, David E. *Daily Life in the United States, 1920–1940: How Americans Lived during the Roaring Twenties and the Great Depression.* Chicago: Ivan R. Dee, 2004.

McElvaine, Robert S. *The Great Depression: America 1929– 1941.* New York: Three Rivers Press, 1993.

Rife, Douglas M. *1929 Stock Market Crash: History in Headlines.* Torrance, Calif.: Good Apple, 2000.

WEB SITES

The Crash of 1929
http://www.btinternet.com/~dreklind/thecrash.htm

Herbert Hoover Presidential Library and Museum
http://hoover.archives.gov/exhibits/Hooverstory/gallery06/ gallery06.html

Looking Back at the Crash of 1929
http://www.nytimes.com/library/financial/index-1929-crash.html

Crash of 1929 Gallery
http://www.pbs.org/wgbh/amex/crash/gallery/index.html

Seeds of the 1929 Crash
http://wsjclassroom.com/archive/02nov/ECON3.htm

PICTURE CREDITS

INDEX

ABOUT THE AUTHOR

BRENDA LANGE has been a journalist, author, and public relations professional for 20 years. During that time, she has written for newspapers, magazines, trade publications, and performed public relations functions for a diverse clientele. She has written or revised six books for Chelsea House. Brenda is a member of the American Society of Journalists and Authors and lives and works in Doylestown, Pennsylvania. Her Web site is *www. brendalange.com.*